Hot Flash Hell

A GYNECOLOGIST'S GUIDE TO TURNING DOWN THE HEAT

D0556332

By Lauren Streicher, MD

Contents

PART 3. INSIDE INFORMATION RESOURCES

Chapter 16
CALLING DR. GOOGLE?

Scroll the web and you're likely to be bombarded with a plethora of advice and products that promise to remove wrinkles, tighten your vagina, cure incontinence, and ensure orgasmic ecstasy. Know how to navigate!

Chapter 17
FINDING A MENOPAUSE TEAM

How to know if the person to whom you are about to bare your soul—and your vagina—is an expert in your problem

Chapter 18
RESOURCES

Chapter 19
TERMINOLOGY/GLOSSARY

ACKNOWLEDGMENTS

INDEX

This book is not intended to replace medical advice and should be used to supplement, not replace care by your personal health care clinician.

The author and the publisher disclaim liability for any medical outcomes that may occur as a result of applying methods suggested or discussed in this book.

HOT FLASH HELL: A Gynecologists Guide to Turning Down the Heat

For information or permission, contact WUDT Press, info@BigThings.com

Book cover, Francey, designed by Joe Darrow.

ISBN: 9798463088598

About Lauren Streicher, MD, FACOG, NCMP

DR. LAUREN STREICHER is a best-selling author, a clinical professor of obstetrics and gynecology at Northwestern University's Feinberg School of Medicine, a certified menopause practitioner of the North American Menopause Society, and the medical director of the Northwestern Medicine Center for Menopause and the Northwestern Medicine Center for Sexual Medicine.

In addition to her consumer books and articles, she has authored multiple scientific publications. Dr. Streicher is routinely interviewed as a reliable, accurate source for national publications such as The New York Times, Newsweek, the Associated Press, and dozens of magazines. She writes regularly for Prevention magazine and The Ethel from AARP.

She was the 2019 recipient of the North American Menopause Society Media Award and has been honored with numerous other recognitions, including annual inclusion on Castle Connolly's Top Doctor Listing.

Dr. Streicher is the medical correspondent for Chicago's top-rated news program, the WGN Morning News, and has appeared multiple times on Today, Good Morning America, The Oprah Winfrey Show, CNN, NPR, Dr. Radio, Nightline, The Dr. Oz Show, Fox and Friends, The Steve Harvey Show, CBS This Morning, ABC News Now, NBC Nightly News, 20/20, and World News Tonight.

She lives in Chicago with her writer-producer husband, Jason Brett, and their dog, KJ. They have four grown daughters.

Other books by Dr. Streicher:

Slip Sliding Away: Turning Back the Clock on Your Vagina
WUDT Press
The Essential Guide to Hysterectomy
1st edition M. Evans & Company
2nd edition M. Evans & Company
Sex Rx: Hormones, Health and Your Best Sex Ever
Harper Collins (originally released as *Love Sex Again*)

To my husband Jason

and

To all the Franceys in the world

Introduction
DR. STREICHER'S INSIDE INFORMATION SERIES

IF EVERY MAN woke up on his 50th birthday and started having all-day, all-night hot flashes, couldn't think, and couldn't function, if his bones started to deteriorate at an alarming rate, if his risk for heart disease dramatically increased, if his penis shrank to the size of a breakfast sausage, and if he were incapable of any sexual activity, he would not be told, "This is a normal part of aging." He would be given solutions. Lots of them.

Yet the 80% of menopausal women who experience symptoms that impede their ability to think, sleep, work, and function sexually are expected to put up with hot flashes, vaginal dryness, weight gain, and insomnia. For most women, this occurs when they are at the prime of their professional and personal lives, but these changes can happen even earlier if someone enters menopause as a result of chemotherapy, radiation, medication, or surgery.

Hot flashes result in an inflammatory response that accelerates vascular changes that lead to heart disease, stroke, and other serious medical conditions.

So it's not just quality of life—it is also length of life.

Many women assume that menopause is temporary, and once the hot flashes go away, menopause is over. But menopause is never over. You do not go through menopause. You enter menopause. Even if you are no longer having hot flashes, the impact of no longer producing estrogen is forever.

It doesn't have to be this way. There are safe, effective treatments that most women are not offered and are not aware of that will protect their bones, their bladder, their brain, their heart, their sex life, and their sanity.

I am solutions-driven, and my mission is to address this enormous, unmet need by giving women good information so they can make good choices. That's why I decided to write my Inside Information Series as a collection of guides that will enable you to navigate the individual issues you are trying to fix. You may end up reading the whole series, or just one book.

Hot Flash Hell: A Gynecologist's Guide to Turning Down the Heat is specifically about hot flashes. After walking you through everything you need to know about what to expect, how to know if you are in perimenopause or menopause, and the impact of those flashes, I will do a deep dive into all the hormonal and nonhormonal options to alleviate those frequent surges of heat.

Every once in a while, someone will say, "My grandmother didn't take anything for hot flashes. Why should I?" Well, Grandma was more likely to be home baking cookies than doing a job that required a good night's sleep and the ability to think clearly. Grandma was unlikely to be starting a second marriage or a new relationship in her 50s. Grandma likely did not live nearly as long as you will.

So, to that end, meet Francey.

FRANCEY'S PERIMENOPAUSE SAGA began in Slip Sliding Away-Turning Back the Clock on Your Vagina, when, like millions of perimenopausal and menopausal women across the country, Francey reentered the dating world only to discover that her vagina had pretty much gone on strike. After successfully solving her problem, she became quite the vagina evangelist, explaining to anyone who would listen that everyone's dry genitals are fixable whether it is with a little lube, a lot of laser, rings, creams, or other things.

While grateful that her vagina is now back in business, she now realizes that she needs to personally get back in business-as in getting a job. Her ex had impressively squandered all their savings investing in a gerbil gymnasium startup. So after 20 years of being an at-home mom, she now needs to make some money.

But, sadly for Francey, her re-entry into the workforce happens to coincide with her entry into hot flash hell. Follow Francey as she explores lifestyle, non-hormonal, and hormonal options to find a solution to her all-day all-night flashes before losing her job, her ability to function, and her mind.

Part 1

THE COLD FACTS ABOUT HOT FLASHES

AFTER A FEW MONTHS of frenzied job searches and cleaning 300 gerbil gymnasiums out of her basement, Francey suddenly realizes that it's been a while since her last period. In a moment of panic because she hadn't used a condom with the hottie she'd met at the gym (what was his name anyway?), she makes a midnight run to the drugstore to purchase three pregnancy tests. The directions say to wait until morning, but it is all she can do to wait until she gets home. All negative. The pregnancy gods have given her a pass.

Francey mentions her lack of periods to her friend Shari, who laughingly tells her that perimenopause is a lot more likely than pregnancy. Francey, convinced that Shari is mistaken, is sure her missing menses is due to a bug or, more likely, stress over not having a job..

1

COULD IT BE... PERIMENOPAUSE? MENOPAUSE? SOME OTHER PAUSE?

MENOPAUSE. THE VERY WORD evokes emotions and re-actions unlike those associated with any other life transi-tion. For many women, menopause symbolizes the end of fertility, femininity, sexuality, and even their very identity. The negative connotation is troublesome, as menopause actually represents liberation. Consider that prehistoric women experienced only 50 menstrual cycles in a lifetime (due to a shorter lifespan and increased rate of pregnancy) as opposed to the approximately 450 menstrual periods ex-perienced by most women today. It's exhausting.

The entry into menopause should represent a time when a woman is not only at her personal and professional peak, but she also can *finally* enjoy life without dealing with PMS, pads, and menstrual cramps. But unlike puberty, when your mother sat you down and explained what to expect with your first period, it is the rare mother who tells her daughter what to expect from her first hot flash, what to do about it, or even what menopause is. In fairness to moms everywhere, no one explained it to them.

So here goes...

In the simplest of terms, menopause is when your estrogen tank is on empty.

The ovaries have permanently stopped producing estrogen or have been surgically removed. Medically, the arrival of menopause is determined retrospectively, when a woman has not had a period for 12 months. But what about all the women who haven't used a tampon for years because of a hysterectomy, endometrial ablation, or an IUD? In addition, it's not as if your periods turn off like a faucet. So it's not always so simple. Chapter 2 will get into the specifics of *how* to know you are in menopause.

Many women assume that once the hot flashes go away, menopause is officially over. That is not the case. Although *some* symptoms of menopause are temporary, the inability to produce estrogen is permanent. Once you are done having hot flashes, the repercussion of your ovaries no longer producing estrogen continues to affect every cell in your body, which is part of the reason your post-menopause heart, vagina, bones, brain, and bladder are not the same as when you were 20.

"You do not go through menopause—you enter menopause"

Once you have officially entered menopause, you can no longer spontaneously get pregnant unless you opt for a fertility treatment using a donor egg. It's not that there are no eggs left, and, in fact, a common misconception is that menopause occurs when a woman runs out of eggs.

Women are born with 1 million to 2 million eggs—far more than they will ever use. And even though women do lose eggs throughout their life, by the time menopause occurs, the average woman still has roughly 300 to 400 eggs remaining, but they are old, useless eggs. So there you have it. Menopause means your ovaries are out of business.

What determines **the age of menopause?**
In the United States, the average time to enter **spontaneous menopause** is 52, but anytime between the ages of 40 and 58 is normal. Most women enter menopause spontaneously, but others enter an **induced menopause** because of chemotherapy, pelvic radiation, medication, or surgery. And that can happen at any age.

There are specific definitions **for those women who are not on the "average" spectrum**
Early Menopause
Although it is normal for a woman to go through menopause in her early 40s, that occurs spontaneously in only 3% to 5% of women. A woman who enters menopause between the ages of 40 and 45 is normal, but it is an early menopause. Most early menopause is induced because of surgery or cancer treatment.

Premature Menopause
Premature menopause occurs at or before the age of 40. In many cases it is genetic, but it may also be the result of an autoimmune disease or be induced by surgery or cancer treatments.

Primary Ovarian Insufficiency
Primary ovarian insufficiency (POI) is defined as when the ovaries temporarily wind down before the age of 40. POI is often confused with premature menopause, which is permanent, but with POI, ovarian activity kicks in again.

Factors that determine the age of menopause
So why is it that some women enter menopause at 44 and others are still getting their period at 55?

The main thing that influences when you go through menopause is genetics. If your mom and older sister were still using tampons in their mid-50s, there is a good chance you will be too. The data is variable regarding ethnicity, but there are studies that suggest that Hispanic American and Black American women tend to enter menopause earlier than Caucasian American and Japanese American women.

Genetics aside, menopause tends to occur earlier in smokers and women with autoimmune diseases such as hypothyroidism, rheumatoid arthritis, and type 1 diabetes.

Contrary to popular belief, the age at which you started menstruating does not determine when you will stop.

Factors associated with an earlier menopause:
- Smoking.
- Autoimmune diseases such as type 1 diabetes and rheumatoid arthritis.
- Night-shift work.
- Hysterectomy, even if the ovaries are not removed.
- Genetic disorders.

Factors associated with a later menopause:
- Alcohol consumption.
- Prior use of birth control pills.
- Higher educational level.
- Higher weight.

So, practically speaking, your adult reproductive life phases are divided into:

Pre-menopause: Starts with puberty and continues until perimenopause. A 15-year-old is pre-menopause.

Perimenopause: The time leading up to menopause, when hormones start to fluctuate, and periods are unpredictably irregular. Any symptoms experienced during menopause can occur during perimenopause. Perimenopause can last weeks, months, or years, but it is officially over when a menstruating woman has been without a period for 12 months. Women who have an induced menopause do not go through perimenopause.

Post-menopause: Life after you enter menopause. You are post-menopause until you die.

But First: Welcome to Perimenopause!

WHEN FRANCEY GETS HER PERIOD two weeks later (of course, while wearing white and about to start a tennis game), she grabs an extra sock from her bag, stuffs it into her crotch, and prays it will stay put. Despite the inconvenience of an unexpected period, she is relieved that she is still getting them.

But after a sleepless night reading about irregular periods in 49-year-old women, she finally accepts that perimenopause is not only possible, but is probable.

Years before estrogen production completely shuts down, hormone levels start to fluctuate wildly during that special time of life known as perimenopause. It is truly unfair that just around the time the kids are finally out of the house and life is looking pretty good, women crash into perimenopausal mood swings, insomnia, vaginal dryness, weight gain, and hot flashes. If you are thinking that sounds a lot like menopause, you are correct. Perimenopausal hormonal fluctuations result in the same symptoms that many women experience when they are in full menopause, with some bonus symptoms such as irregular and unpredictable bleeding patterns and exaggerated PMS symptoms like breast tenderness and bloating.

> *The only thing that is predictable is that your period generally arrives as you get on a plane wearing white and carrying no tampons.*

Two specific things differentiate perimenopause from menopause.

1. In perimenopause, your estrogen tank is not yet on permanent empty, and your ovaries may decide to jump back into action. Typically, your symptoms disappear immediately after you spend a month's salary on remedies that claim to eradicate hot flashes and mood swings (sometimes even before you take the new products out of the bag), because perimenopausal symptoms often come and go without treatment. So it's not that the black cohosh worked; it's that your ovaries have kicked in for one last hurrah.

2. Periods are often irregular and unpredictable during perimenopause, but *once in menopause, you no longer get periods.*

These hormonal fluctuations may last months... or years. And, yes, it is normal to start as early as when you blow out the candles on your 40th birthday cake. A 2021 study of over 2400 women aged 35 to 55 years reported that women not only were having these symptoms while still menstruating, but were surprised that they were experiencing them since they did not expect perimenopause to interfere with their daily lives until age 50.

Once you are in menopause, symptoms do not come and go. In fact, if a woman starts having flashes after she has been flash-free for years, low estrogen is unlikely to be the culprit.

An infection, medications, endocrinologic disease, neurologic disease, cancer, sleep apnea, and alcohol use are all on the list of possibilities. An internist or endocrinologist is your go-to specialist to evaluate non-menopause-related hot flashes or night sweats.

Second **Puberty?**

The popular saying "perimenopause is like a second puberty" could not be further from the truth. Puberty is a miserable rite of passage. But acne and irregular periods are not associated with life-threatening and life-shortening changes to the cardiovascular system and bones. Nor is puberty associated with the inability to think or get a decent night's sleep.

***Puberty** heralds the beginning of the reproductive years, when women have high levels of estrogen to support not only their reproductive system, but also their brain, bones, and heart.*

***Perimenopause,** on the other hand, heralds the beginning of a time when women must take steps to ensure their health and longevity.*

Perimenopause can last months or years and officially morphs into menopause when a woman has been without a period for 12 months, but it's not as if menopause arrives and the symptoms go away. In other words, hot flashes and insomnia may last for 10 years or more—vaginal dryness until death. Sorry.

Waiting out bothersome hot flashes, mood swings, and insomnia is not generally the best strategy seeing as perimenopause can last for years. So before I get into the meat of this book, which is the elimination of hot flashes, what about controlling perimenopausal symptoms?

The Pill and Perimenopause

It is a common occurrence for a woman in our menopause clinic to complain that her doctor "just wanted to put me on the pill." For many women, it is not only the right thing to do but also the best thing to do.

Perimenopausal women are experiencing wildly fluctuating hormonal shifts. The birth control pill suppresses ovarian function and supplies a steady dose of estrogen and progesterone. The pill is a convenient and effective form of perimenopausal hormone therapy and is a way of saying to the ovaries, "You seem confused, so we'll take it from here."

Birth control pills should be labeled "hormone control pills."

I can't tell you how many of my patients happily take the pill but then balk at the idea of taking hormone therapy when they stop because of the common misconception that the pill is safe, but hormone therapy is dangerous. Most women are shocked to learn that their "low-dose" birth control pill has far more potent levels of estrogen, and far more potential side effects, than menopausal hormone therapy.

So, given that the pill is a form of hormone therapy, or HT, why not just start menopausal doses of HT instead of putting a 46-year-old woman on birth control pills?

Two reasons:

- Some 46-year-old women are still at risk of getting pregnant (low fertility is not the same as no fertility!), and menopausal HT is not contraception.
- Even more important, women who have fluctuating hormones and are still getting periods will often have irregular bleeding if they take HT because it is too low of a dose to suppress ovarian function.

Medical experts agree that it is safe for low-risk, non-smoking women to stay on birth control pills up to age 55. Ninety percent of women are in menopause by their mid-50s and then can transition to lower-dose hormone therapy.

No Period? No Problem!

I always advise women who are on the pill to take it continuously, meaning no fake pills, no pill-free days, and best of all, no period. Think about it: If you take birth control pills to control perimenopausal hormonal fluctuations, not only is it OK to skip the hormone-free days, but it makes more sense. The goal is to avoid hormonal fluctuations, and the best way to do that is to expose your body to the same amount of hormones every single day.

Some women worry that it is medically a problem to not get a period on the pill. When the pill was first released for use as a contraceptive in 1960, it was prescribed to include a hormone-free week to ensure a normal menstrual period not because it was medically necessary, but because the scientists who invented it felt that maintaining a normal menstrual cycle would make women comfortable with taking this new form of contraception.

The truth is, there is, and never was, *a medical benefit* to that week off, and there are several medical advantages (beyond wearing white pants without fear) to skipping the pill-free intervals and take an active pill 365 days a year.

For the perimenopausal woman, taking a pill continuously means smooth sailing: no hormonal fluctuations, irregular bleeding, crazy PMS symptoms, or unpredictable hot flashes. Kind of like cheating, but why not?

Taking your birth control pill continuously is fine for perimenopausal women, and it is also appropriate for women of any age, so tell your daughters. This approach has the tampon companies in a panic, but I digress.

Other strategies to alleviate perimenopausal symptoms

If you are not a candidate for the pill, or simply prefer not to take it, there are many other ways to control perimenopausal symptoms. The approach depends specifically on what symptoms you are having and where you are in your perimenopause journey. Any hormone therapy (estrogen and/or progesterone) can be used but is generally prescribed cyclically instead of continuously to avoid irregular bleeding.

Irregular periods: Many women who prefer not to take the pill do very well with a progesterone intrauterine device or supplement with oral progesterone. Others just live with irregular periods if they are not too bothersome. Irregular bleeding is not unusual during perimenopause and is usually not an indication of a problem. Having said that, *heavy or frequent bleeding should be checked out to make sure there is not something else going on.* Any bleeding that occurs once you have gone 12 months without a period is abnormal and needs to be evaluated.

Perimenopausal hot flashes: During perimenopause, these can be treated using any of the options described in the rest of the book.

Perimenopausal vaginal dryness: All the strategies discussed in *Slip Sliding Away: Turning Back the Clock on Your Vagina* can be implemented during perimenopause.

The most important thing about perimenopause is to understand what is going on. This is the time to educate yourself about what is happening in your body and to be aware of coming attractions: in other words, menopause. Eventually, when your ovaries permanently stop producing estrogen, perimenopause will morph into menopause.

Here's the important part:

With life expectancy well into the 80s or even 90s, women spend at least one-third of their life after the menopause transition.

There is no reason that any woman should spend years putting up with hot flashes, vaginal dryness, weight gain, and insomnia. Not to mention, given the number of years that follow the menopause transition, it is critically important to protect your bones, your brain, your heart, your sex life, and your sanity.

But I think I can safely assume that if you are reading this, you are currently experiencing Hot Flash Hell and are looking for solutions. And you have probably already figured out that if your doctor has assured you that this is a normal part of aging and you should just tough it out, it's time to find a new doctor. So read on.

OVER COCKTAILS, Francey grills Shari about the details of her perimenopause journey. Evidently, Shari had a hysterectomy at age 40 (who knew!) and there was no "journey". In fact, she wasn't sure if she was in perimenopause or just crabby and sleepless because her boss was driving her crazy. By the third round of Cosmopolitans, Francey still has no clue if she is perimenopausal, and more important, if she should keep buying tampons.

2

IS IT MENOPAUSE OR MIDLIFE?

IN A PERFECT WORLD, an alert would pop up on your phone announcing, "You are now in perimenopause," followed at the appropriate time by "You are now leaving perimenopause and entering menopause." Are you listening, Apple people?

Making the diagnosis can be tricky. If you are 43 years old and your periods are no longer regular, perimenopause is one possibility but not the only possibility. Is your weight gain a consequence of menopause, middle age, or a thyroid that's out of whack? Are your irregular periods because of fluctuating hormones, stress, illness, or medication? Is your vulvar itching because you are dry or because you have a skin condition such as lichen sclerosus? Are you moody because your hormones are out of whack or because you just lost your job, your husband is having an affair, your kid just came home with another piercing, and you are dealing with a 20-pound weight gain? Or all the above?

Thyroid problems, pituitary issues, various medications, and many medical conditions are all on the list. By the way, so is pregnancy. During perimenopause, fertility diminishes. But again, *low fertility* is not the same as *no fertility*, so thinking about contraception may still be on the agenda. And, yes, hot flashes can be caused by conditions other than menopause.

Figuring Out Whether You Have Entered Menopause
If You Don't Get Periods

If the hallmark early warning sign that hormones are shifting is irregular periods and perimenopause extends until someone has not had a period for a full year, what about the woman who doesn't menstruate? Those parameters are meaningless for the millions of midlife women who don't get periods.

Hysterectomy

Thirty percent of women in the United States have had their uterus removed. Keep in mind that *the uterus* does not make estrogen, so if the ovaries are not removed, a hysterectomy will not initiate menopause. It is only if ovaries are removed at the time of hysterectomy and a woman is not already in menopause, she will enter surgical menopause. Post-hysterectomy, you will no longer get periods, and you will not be able to get pregnant, but, again, unless your ovaries were removed, nothing will change hormonally.

I also want to mention that many women undergo a hysterectomy in their 40s or early 50s, and even if their ovaries are not removed, they enter menopause shortly after, not because of the hysterectomy, but because that is when they were destined to go into menopause. It's a coincidence.

Having said that, there is scientific evidence that women who undergo a hysterectomy, even without ovary removal, may go through an earlier, spontaneous menopause than if they had not had a hysterectomy. It's not clear why that is but it may be related to decreased blood flow to the ovaries that occurs because of the surgery.

Endometrial Ablation

Endometrial ablation is a surgical procedure in which a device is used to destroy the inner lining of the uterus (the part that bleeds every month) to control heavy or irregular bleeding. While women who have had an endometrial ablation often no longer get periods, this procedure does not impact hormones. Women post-ablation go through menopause at whatever time they are destined to do so; they just might not know it.

Progesterone IUDs

Many women in their 40s opt for an intrauterine device (IUD) for contraception or to control heavy periods. Up to 50% of women with a progesterone IUD don't get periods, even though they are still making plenty of estrogen.

Birth Control Pills

Women in the 40- to 50-year-old range (prime time for perimenopause) commonly use hormonal contraception, such as a birth control pill, ring, or patch, not only to prevent pregnancy but also to manage perimenopausal symptoms and heavy or irregular periods, as mentioned in chapter 1.

The ovaries are essentially on hiatus if a woman is taking the pill, which means that a period—or lack of a period—is NOT an indication of ovarian function or estrogen output. Even if a woman is taking her pill cyclically and has a light monthly period, the disappearance of her period is not an indication of menopause. It is an indication that the lining of her uterus is thin and inactive because of taking the pill. In other words, it's the pill talking, not the ovaries.

Is it possible for someone to enter menopause while on the pill? Absolutely. Many women continue taking birth control pills until they are 55 and go through perimenopause without even knowing it. Women who are on the pill during perimenopause or menopause do not get hot flashes because the pill is HORMONE THERAPY! The only indication a woman on the pill has that she is going through perimenopause is if she takes the pill cyclically (meaning she does not take an active pill every day) and notices hot flashes during the pill-free days.

FOUR MONTHS of no periods later, Francey happens to be at her internist to get a blood pressure check (high blood pressure runs in her family) and mentions that she thinks she might be perimenopausal. In addition to her lack of periods, she is also occasionally waking up in a pool of sweat. Her internist offers to check her hormone levels, and even though she kind of doesn't really want to know, it seems like a good idea given her symptoms.

The next day her internist calls and assures her that her hormone levels are perfectly normal, and she is not perimenopausal!

Based on her bloodwork, she figures it is worth investing in the jumbo box of tampons on her next trip to Costco.

Time for a Blood Test?

So, what about measuring hormone levels? I can't tell you how many times a woman will come to me and tell me that she thinks she is in perimenopause, but her internist did a hormone test and told her she was not. In most cases, the woman is right, and the internist was wrong.

Here's why: Typically, the hormone levels that are measured are FSH and estradiol.

Follicle-stimulating hormone (FSH) is a hormone produced by the pituitary gland, which is located at the base of the brain. FSH stimulates the production of estrogen by the ovaries and during the reproductive years stimulates the growth of ovarian follicles (the small cysts that hold the eggs).

During perimenopause, FSH levels fluctuate. Once a woman has entered menopause and estrogen production has ceased, FSH levels remain high.

Estradiol, also called 17β-estradiol, is the most potent of the naturally occurring estrogens and is the primary estrogen produced by the ovaries during the reproductive years. Estradiol levels rise and fall during a normal menstrual cycle and fluctuate unpredictably during perimenopause.

Testing your blood hormone level to check for pituitary function (FSH) and estrogen levels will be an accurate measure of your hormones at 2:00 p.m. on Tuesday, when your blood was drawn, but may be completely different one week later. One random level is not a reliable indication of the total picture. Sometimes serial blood levels are helpful (around two weeks apart) but not definitive. If you are taking hormonal contraception, any blood test is worthless, because it is the pill supplying estrogen, not your ovaries.

Anti-Mullerian Hormone (AMH)

Sometimes *Anti-Mullerian Hormone* is measured as a predictor of when someone is going to go into menopause, using algorithms that include age and other factors, such as smoking and obesity. AMH is secreted by cells from follicles in the ovaries. Follicles are present only if healthy eggs are still around. AMH declines with age, as the "good" egg pool declines and is completely gone after menopause.

Blood levels of anti-mullerian hormone have been used by fertility specialists for years to evaluate a woman's ovarian reserve—essentially how good her eggs are and how long they will be functional.

But these measures have not been found to be reliable when it comes to menopause. Like FSH and estradiol, AMH levels may fluctuate and can be misleading. Although some clinicians may obtain an AMH reading to see if a woman has entered menopause, it is only useful if it is zero. Remember: AMH does not measure estrogen levels; it is an indicator of egg quality.

Home Menopause Tests

If you can do a home pregnancy test, why not a home menopause test? I'll tell you why not: They are pretty much worthless. These over-the-counter tests measure FSH in urine and claim to be 99% accurate. And that is true: They are 99% accurate in detecting the presence of FSH in urine. FSH rises after a woman enters menopause, but FSH also goes up every time a woman ovulates. Again, during midlife, FSH levels fluctuate widely, especially if you are having irregular periods, mood swings that come and go, and on-and-off hot flashes—in other words, perimenopause. Save your money.

Saliva Testing

Most people expect to pee in a cup when they visit their doctor, but spit in a cup? Alternative practitioners originally popularized salivary testing as a way to measure hormone levels and determine the dosage of compounded menopausal hormone therapy. The practice finally started to fall out of favor around 10 years ago as awareness increased that saliva was not a valid way to diagnose menopause or individualize hormone therapy. I thought I was through explaining to patients that the hundreds and sometimes thousands of dollars they had spent on saliva analysis were essentially wasted, but occasionally, a patient presents me with pages of saliva testing results to be included as an integral part of their medical record. So, what's going on?

It all started when the late Dr. John Lee promoted the idea of salivary hormone testing in his bestseller, *Hormone Balance Made Simple*. Although Dr. Lee died in 2003, his work (and website, book, products, etc.) live on. His website in 2021 states, *"Knowing your saliva hormone levels is an important first step in assessing where your hormones may be out of balance. ... [R]esearch indicates that the most accurate way to do so is through saliva."* To his credit, the very small print at the bottom of the page does acknowledge that his home hormone-testing products (sold for the low, low price of $255) *"are not offered for the diagnosis, cure, mitigation, treatment, or prevention of any disease or disorder, nor have any statements herein been evaluated by the Food and Drug Administration (FDA)."*

Now, no one argues that estrogen and progesterone levels are detectable in saliva, and it would be great if a drop of spit could unravel the mysteries of menopause. Unfortunately, although there are still practitioners eager to take your saliva and your money, salivary hormone levels have not been proven useful in any scientific studies when it comes to making a diagnosis of menopause or determining the necessity for, or the appropriate dosage of, hormone replacement.

Not only is there absolutely no scientific evidence that saliva levels correlate to blood levels or response to treatment, but salivary hormone levels also vary depending on diet, the time of day the testing was conducted, and many other variables. The American College of Obstetrics and Gynecology issued a bulletin in 2005 stating that hormone levels in saliva are not biologically meaningful and are not recommended. So save your money and your saliva.

THREE WEEKS LATER, still no period, and now her night sweats (followed by shivering spells) are back with a vengeance. For the first time, Francey is grateful that she is not sharing her bed with anyone because she is not only a sweaty mess but also up and down all night. After doing a little more midnight internet research, she decides that because perimenopause isn't her problem (according to her internist), her night sweats must be from lymphoma or HIV.

Fortunately, she has a scheduled appointment with her new gynecologist, Dr. Herpes (you'd think she would have changed her name when she picked her specialty, Francey thinks). The doctor explains why Francey's hormone blood tests were "misleading" (carefully avoiding words like "worthless" and "pointless") and tells her that she is in perimenopause as opposed to having some dreaded disease. She goes on to say that Francey's blood pressure is now officially in the too-high range, and on the way out of the room, she mentions that her name is pronounced "Hare-pay."

How I Diagnose Menopause

I know this sounds old school, but the best way for me to know if someone is in perimenopause or menopause is to listen to her story: What is she experiencing, and how long has she been experiencing it? The best indicator that you are no longer making estrogen is how you feel. The fact that you are having hot flashes, vaginal dryness, mood swings, or insomnia and can't remember why you walked into a room is a better indication that you are perimenopausal than any laboratory test with the caveat that there is nothing else going on, like thyroid dysfunction. It's not rocket science to figure out when a patient tells me her last period was two years ago, her vagina is like the Sahara Desert, and she has nonstop hot flashes that she is officially in menopause. I don't need a blood test to prove that a 55-year-old woman who hasn't had a period in three years has low estrogen. It's kind of like getting a pregnancy test for someone who is in labor and being surprised that it is positive.

Once I eliminate other medical problems that may cause similar signs, I make the diagnosis based on age and sometimes blood work, but mostly I make the diagnosis based on symptoms.

Menopause Symptoms

About 20% of women have no symptoms, but those women are not reading this book. Hot flashes are the number one symptom that women associate with menopause and, though they are not exactly welcome, they are at least expected. And yet a surprising number of otherwise-savvy women are not aware of the association between lack of estrogen and their other symptoms.

The following list does not even come close to including every possible symptom a woman might experience—just the most common ones. It also does not include the consequences of menopause, such as bone loss.

Genital and urinary tract symptoms
- Painful (or impossible) intercourse.
- Vulvar itching.
- Vulvar burning.
- Orgasms that are easier to fake than experience.
- That constant "gotta go" feeling.
- Recurrent urinary tract infections.
- Vaginal dryness that a bucketful of lube doesn't help.
- Thinning or disappearing labia.

Symptoms related to or a consequence of all-night-and-day hot flashes
- Inability to concentrate.
- Inability to remember why you walked into a room.
- Palpitations.
- Weight gain.
- Anxiety that goes beyond the terrifying state of the world.
- Sleepless nights.
- Fatigue (kind of expected if you never sleep).
- Mood swings and irritability.
- A nonexistent libido.

Everything else
- A muffin top (even if you don't put on a pound).
- Dry, itchy skin (everywhere).
- Formication (feeling of insects crawling on skin).
- Achy joints.
- Thinning hair.
- Wrinkles.
- Depression—beyond being depressed about having all these symptoms.

Every woman's menopause is different. When a woman comes to the Northwestern Medicine menopause center, she starts by filling out a checklist as a way of letting us know what she is experiencing. Because most women check off at least 10 items, we then ask, "What are your most bothersome symptoms? If you could fix only one or two things, what would they be?"

It almost always comes down to the big four:

- **80%** of women say, *"Help me get rid of these **hot flashes.**"*
- **60%** of women say, *"Help me get a **decent night's sleep.**"*
- **60%** of women say, *"Help me get rid of **pain with sex.**"*
- **90%** of women say, *"Help me get rid of **the weight.**"*

What you will learn in subsequent pages is that hot flashes are at least partially responsible for insomnia and weight gain. Painful intercourse is covered in ***Slip Sliding Away: Turning Back the Clock on Your Vagina-A gynecologist's guide to eliminating post-menopause dryness and pain.*** Additional symptoms are covered in other ***Inside Information*** books.

This book is going to stick to hot flashes.

DESPITE HAVING FILLED OUT *multiple applications, there just doesn't seem to be a big demand for a middle-aged, sweating, insomniac who has been out of the workforce for 20 years. Acting on a tip from a friend about a receptionist job at the local art museum, Francey figures she is a shoo-in because she has volunteered there for years. And, bingo, three days after submitting her application, she is asked to come in for an interview.*

Feeling confident about her job interview but also anxious about being labeled "too old," Francey touches up her gray roots and dons the power black pants, cream-colored silk blouse, and the way-overpriced-but-totally-worth-it Louboutin heels she bought at an upscale consignment shop. Midway through her interview, she is suddenly aware that she is experiencing what appears to be an internal furnace. The heat only lasts a few minutes, but a glance in the mirror confirms her worst fear: huge sweat stains on her silk-covered armpits. More than a little distracted, she powers through the rest of the interview and hopes no one notices.

3

HOT FLASH FACTS

MEDICAL DEFINITION OF A HOT FLASH: *A condition resulting in a red, flushed face and neck, sweating, an increase in pulse rate, and a rapid heartbeat, often followed by a cold chill.*

Definition from real-life women and common greeting cards: *Your body deciding to spontaneously combust while taking you on a secret rollercoaster ride through the bowels of hell.*

Hot flashes, the "I'm hot; now I'm cold" thermoregulatory dysfunction that occurs in up to 80% of menopausal women, is a consequence of an inner thermostat that is malfunctioning. The experience of a hot flash is highly variable but generally is some version of the sudden sensation of heat on the face and upper chest that becomes generalized. Sometimes the heat is followed by shivering. A severe flash can be intense (I call it "the furnace inside you"), lasting between two and four minutes.

The Science Behind a Hot Flash
The human body is meant to be roughly 98.6 degrees. If you go outside in the winter without your coat, you're going

to shiver to generate heat. You sweat when you exercise to cool the body down. The part of the brain that keeps your body at the right temperature is known as the thermoregulatory zone, which is located in the hypothalamus. During menopause, the thermoregulatory zone gets too sensitive, resulting in hot flashes even when the body doesn't really need to cool down. To dive a little deeper into the science, the thermoregulatory zone is controlled by the signaling of a receptor known as *neurokinin 3* (NK3), which is controlled by estrogen. This is important because a new, non-hormonal drug that controls this system, fezolinetant, is currently in phase 3 clinical trials. If all goes well, fezolinetant will be available in the next couple of years.

Physiologically, a hot flash happens for the same reason you sweat in a sauna: The body is trying to cool itself down. The difference is that you don't really need to cool down, but your menopausal brain thinks you do.

Science aside, there are four phases to what women experience:

Phase 1: Your core body temperature goes up, the blood vessels in your skin dilate, your skin gets warm, and your heart rate speeds up.

Phase 2: The heat becomes more intense, with reddening of the skin on the upper body.

Phase 3: Your heart rate peaks, and the sweating starts. This is sometimes profuse sweating—like dripping-down-your-back sweating.

Phase 4: The heat wave and shivering are followed by chills as your body tries to cool off.

The medical term for hot flashes is vasomotor symptoms, with "vasomotor" referring to changes in the diameter of your blood vessels that cause you to feel hot, then cold, followed by a racing pulse and anxiety. Has it occurred to you yet that these are the identical biologic responses that occur with fear?

When Do **They Start?**

One in eight women start to experience hot flashes while still getting regular periods, but most experience them once their cycle becomes irregular or menstruation has stopped.

Night sweats that occur before the age of 45 (in a woman who is still menstruating) or years after the onset of menopause are generally not hormonal. Cancer, infection, medications, endocrine causes, neurologic diseases, sleep apnea, and alcohol use are all possible causes of night sweats that have nothing to do with menopause or shifting hormones.

How Many a Day **Is Typical?**

In women who report moderate to severe flashes, the average number is 19.5 per day.

Those with severe flashes experience up to 30 a day. But the key word is "experience." Because here's the headline: It turns out, women have many more flashes than they are aware of.

In research settings, hot flashes are recorded using a skin conductance monitor to objectively measure change in temperature instead of relying on self-reporting. Although there is a lot of variability in terms of how many flashes a woman actually has versus how many flashes she is aware of, in one study, women were subjectively aware of only 36% to 50% of true, monitor-verified hot flashes if awake and between 22% and 42% if asleep. In another study, only 69% of hot flashes were associated with awakening.

The obvious question is, why does it matter how many flashes someone is having if she doesn't know it? The answer is, even flashes you are not aware of can have a negative effect on your heart, cognitive function, and all the other parameters discussed in the next chapter. In addition, it is useful to know how many flashes someone is experiencing so we know if treatment is working. But no one, unless they are part of a study protocol, is going to have an exact count, and you have better things to do than record every flash you have during the day, much less sit up all night.

So what makes sense is to have a general idea of how many flashes you have during the day. One strategy I suggest to my patients to record nighttime flashes is to have a box of facial tissues at the bedside. I tell them that every time they are awakened by a flash, they should throw a piece of tissue on the floor. In the morning, they can count their flashes—or at least the ones that woke them up. This is also a great way to track if whatever you are using to get rid of your hot flashes is working.

Hot Flash **Triggers**
Pretty much anything can trigger a hot flash, including doing nothing. Some women predictably flash when they are stressed (as in, stressed from having a lot of hot flashes), eat spicy foods, drink caffeine, or have a glass of red wine.

And though, theoretically, one can reduce hot flashes by eating tasteless food, giving up your morning latte, and forgoing alcohol, I would rather flash.

Mild, Moderate, **or Severe?**

For some women, hot flashes are extremely debilitating. For others, less so. Women who get warm a few times a day don't understand why others need help to get through menopause. The woman who flashes 20 to 30 times a day, can't sleep, and can't get through a business meeting fully clothed probably coined the bumper-sticker-worthy phrase, "I'm out of estrogen, and I've got a gun."

Hot Flash **Categories**

- *None* – This woman is not reading this book.
- *Mild* – You're aware that you are suddenly a little warm, but flashes do not interfere with your usual activities. Basically, you might take off your sweater.
- *Moderate* – Flashes interfere with your usual activities, and you seriously think about getting naked at work on a regular basis.
- *Severe* – Sweat drips down your back, you can't sleep, you can't think, you can't function, and you hate everyone. And the flashes keep on coming...sometimes 20 to 30 times a day.

AN ANNOUNCEMENT about an informational lecture on menopause sponsored by her local hospital pops up in her Facebook feed (how did they know?!), and she immediately signs up.

Surrounded by sweating, irritable women, including one who has clipped a little battery-operated fan to the chair in front of her, she is shocked to learn just how long she might be supporting her local dry cleaner and getting essentially no sleep.

At the "mocktail" hour after the lecture, Francey connects with Marla, the manager of her favorite shoe store! They ditch the Shirley Temples and head to a hotel bar, where, over way too many martinis, they bond over uplifting topics such as hot flashes, dry vaginas, and ex-husbands.

The next morning, Francey wakes up with a splitting headache, but she's also received a congratulatory email that despite her wet pits, the job is hers!

How Long Do They Last?

Until a few years ago, most doctors (including me) believed that hot flashes lasted only a couple of years, and while acknowledging that they seemed to go on much longer than that for some women, we thought they were outliers. Based on that premise, most women just tough it out under the misconception that the misery won't last more than a few years.

The SWAN study, released in 2015, completely debunked the myth that flashes are fleeting.

I am going to take a minute here to discuss the SWAN study because much of what we now understand about menopause, and much of the information in this book, is derived from SWAN data.

The Study of Women's Health Across the Nation (SWAN) is ongoing research of more than 3,000 midlife women. Starting in 1994, Caucasian (46%), Black (28%), Hispanic (9%), and Asian (17%) American women from all over the country were enrolled in the study between the ages of 40 and 55 to evaluate multiple parameters of midlife health and the impacts of menopause and hormone therapy. This culturally diverse group continues to be seen annually to study the physical, biologic, and psychological aspects of aging. Younger women (pre-menopause) were specifically included to evaluate the impact of menopause.

Some of the areas SWAN is specifically studying include:
- Bone health.
- Depression.
- Stress.
- Sleep.
- Physical functioning.
- Patterns of medication use.
- Sexual health.
- Vaginal health.
- Urinary health.
- Hormonal changes.

The data continues to roll in, and more than any other research, it has increased our knowledge about the effect of aging and menopause on health and has changed the way menopause experts advise and treat midlife women. In addition to studying natural hormonal changes, SWAN data also includes the impact of smoking, diet, medications, hormone therapy, and multiple psychosocial variables on a woman's health.

By 2021, almost 600 scientific studies have been published. If you would like to look at this information yourself, all the studies are published on the SWAN website, www.swanstudy.org.

It is from SWAN data that we know the truth about how long hot flashes last.

On average, hot flashes happen for seven years but can last up to 14 years.

Up to 9% of women continue to have hot flashes for 20 years.

THE MORNING AFTER THE DEMORALIZING hot flash lecture, Francey calls her mom, who has just returned from a hiking trip. It turns out, her mom also had terrible hot flashes, but before she has a chance to ask how long they lasted or what she did to get rid of them, her mom dashes off for her yoga class.

In addition, we learned from SWAN that ethnicity, independent of what kind of food someone eats or their diet and exercise patterns, is a major determinant of the length of time someone is destined to flash.

Black American women: 10 years

Hispanic American women: 8.9 years

Caucasian American women: 6.5 years

Asian American women: 5 years

Genetics, beyond ethnicity, also plays a role. If your mom had flashes that lasted for years, chances are you are also destined to flash for years. Obesity, smoking, and reduced physical activity are also associated with flashes. And the earlier someone goes through menopause, the longer hot flashes last.

AT THIS POINT, Francey accepts that she is in the throes of perimenopause. She crosses her fingers and hopes that she'll be one of the lucky ones whose symptoms last only a few months. Right now, her main priority is to kick ass at her new job.

FRANCEY'S HIGH BLOOD PRESSURE has been on her mind, and because she has a week until her first day of work, she schedules a visit with the cardiologist Dr. Herpes recommended. Her father had his first heart attack in his 40s and died in his early 60s, and she wants to do everything she can to make sure she is not destined for the same fate. She mentions her all-day, all-night hot flashes to the cardiologist, who, much to her shock, tells her that her hot flashes might be driving up her blood pressure. In addition to medication and some changes in her diet, she encourages her to talk to Dr. Herpes about getting her hot flashes under control.

4

THINK YOUR HOT FLASHES WON'T KILL YOU? THINK AGAIN!

EVEN IF YOU ARE WILLING to spend 10 or more years of your life dressing in layers, tossing and turning all night, and carrying a portable fan, the impact of hot flashes goes far beyond the misery of feeling like you are living in a sauna. There is now an abundance of scientific evidence that hot flashes increase your risk of developing cardiovascular disease and other serious medical conditions.

Your Heart on Hot Flashes

Here's what's going on. Every time you have a hot flash, your heart rate increases, and your blood pressure elevates. You are not imagining those palpitations! In other words, hot flashes make your heart work harder.

It also appears that hot flashes cause an inflammatory response, which in turn damages blood vessels. Add a hot flash-induced elevation of LDL-C (the bad cholesterol) and it is no wonder that the risk of heart trouble or stroke is associated with women who experience frequent and persistent hot flashes compared to women who are flash-free, even when you take into consideration other risk factors, such as obesity, smoking, and diabetes.

In the Study of Women's Health Across the Nation (see chapter 3), women who had frequent or persistent hot flashes had a dramatic increase in the risk of heart trouble or stroke over the women who were flash-free.

What About That Study That Said Hormones Were Bad for the Heart?

The current news that eliminating flashes with hormone therapy will decrease the risk of cardiovascular disease is in direct opposition to what women were told in 2002, when the results of the Women's Health Initiative (WHI) were released. The WHI was a large study with the purpose of definitively determining whether long-term hormone therapy could prevent heart disease and prolong life. Post-WHI, women were advised to abandon hormone therapy because the study determined it would increase the risk of heart disease and stroke. The details are in chapter 14.

But more than 70% of the women enrolled in the WHI were over the age of 60. Most of them were no longer having hot flashes, which meant the damage to their blood vessels was already done by the time they started hormone therapy. Because most women go through menopause between the ages of 45 and 55 (representing less than 10% of the WHI study population), the overall results were reflective of women who were well past the hot flash years. In other words, *the damage to their heart had already occurred.*

An evaluation of the study looking only at women in the 50- to 60-year-old range showed completely different and very reassuring results. There was actually a decrease in coronary heart disease and a 30% decrease in overall mortality in women who were taking estrogen. Was that decrease simply because they were taking estrogen? Or was it because the estrogen eliminated their hot flashes? Impossible to determine, but given what we know now, I suspect it was because estrogen eliminated their hot flashes as opposed to the benefits being a direct effect of estrogen.

That's right: Although diabetes, obesity, elevated blood pressure, and smoking are recognized risk factors, it appears that hot flashes are also on the list of culprits that contribute to the development of heart disease.

Hot Flashes Are Associated with the Following Cardiovascular Risk Factors

- Elevated cortisol.
- Increase in inflammatory markers.
- Blood vessel damage (atherosclerosis).
- Increased LDL cholesterol.
- Increased blood pressure.
- Increased heart rate.
- Increased aortic calcification.

Cardiovascular Disease Is Not the Only Condition Impacted by Hot Flashes

Every time you have a hot flash, you increase your cortisol and initiate an inflammatory response, resulting in damage to blood vessels throughout the body. Every organ system is affected.

Osteoporosis

In a study of over 5,600 women ages 46 to 57, bone loss correlated with the frequency of hot flashes, even when age, weight, smoking, hormone therapy, exercise, and other risk factors were taken into consideration. In the United States alone, there are 8 million women with osteoporosis and 34 million women with low bone mass (osteopenia) who are at risk of fracture and don't know it. By age 80, 50% of women have osteoporosis and are at significant risk of fracture if they fall. Fractures from osteoporosis are responsible for 2 million fractures per year. Twenty-five percent of women over age 50 die because of osteoporotic hip fracture. Osteoporosis is not just about getting shorter.

Breast Cancer
Breast cancer is the most common cancer in females in the United States and the second-most-common cause of cancer death in women. Though there are many factors that increase (or decrease) the risk, in the Study of Women's Health Across the Nation, or SWAN, the 13-year follow-up showed a whopping 50% increased risk of breast cancer in women with moderate to severe hot flashes. It's not just the severity of hot flashes; it is also how long they last. Women that had flashes lasting 10 years or longer had a higher incidence of breast cancer than women with short-term hot flashes.

This is thought to be one of the reasons there is a 23% decrease in breast cancer in women using estrogen therapy. (More on this in chapter 14) Think about that: The majority of women who avoid estrogen do so because they think it will increase their risk of breast cancer when, in fact, the opposite is true.

Diabetes
Insulin is the hormone produced by the pancreas that controls blood sugar metabolism. In adults who have type 2 diabetes, the body does not respond to normal amounts of insulin (insulin resistance) and requires the pancreas to produce progressively higher amounts. Controlling type 2 diabetes is important to avoid complications such as

cardiovascular disease. SWAN data shows that women who have hot flashes have an increase in insulin resistance, which in turn increases their risk of developing diabetes or may potentially sabotage their efforts to manage diabetes if they already have it.

But there's more. The next chapter gets into the effect of hot flashes on sleep, weight control, and cognition.

FIRST DAY OF WORK. With her sweaty hot flashes and unpredictable bleeding, Francey realizes that wearing layers of black isn't as much of a fashion statement anymore as it is an "I'm in perimenopause" statement.

Two weeks into the job, her hot flashes seem to have abated, and even a particularly heavy surprise period just as 30 out-of-control second graders arrive for a field trip doesn't slow her down. Fortunately, she is carrying her "just in case" tampons and wearing head-to-toe black. She is finally feeling confident about life in general and her ability to succeed at the museum.

5

ARE YOUR HOT FLASHES MAKING YOU FAT? FOGGY? FORGETFUL?

IT'S THE RARE WOMAN who arrives at our menopause clinic and says, "Now that I have entered menopause, I am really worried about my risk of stroke." Heart disease, osteoporosis, and diabetes are just not things women are thinking about when they make an appointment.

What gets women in the door, beyond hot flashes, are the out-of-control weight gain, memory issues, and inability to sleep. And guess what: The women who are having those symptoms are the same ones who are flashing. Women with vaginal dryness (who are not also having hot flashes) are generally not the ones struggling to get into their pants. It turns out that though hot flashes are not the whole story, they are a major contributor not only to weight gain but also to problems with cognitive function and sleep.

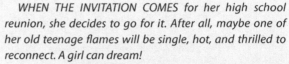

WHEN THE INVITATION COMES for her high school reunion, she decides to go for it. After all, maybe one of her old teenage flames will be single, hot, and thrilled to reconnect. A girl can dream!

In preparation for said amazing guy, she digs out an old go-to dress.

A quick check in the mirror and she's shocked that, instead of herself, she sees her mother staring back at her, including the huge lump around her midsection, and—horrors—the zipper will not zip.

Francey waits to weigh herself until the next morning, tentatively stepping on the scale before she eats anything and after she pees. She's taken aback by a number that's 7 pounds over her "acceptable" weight and 10 pounds over her "ideal" weight. She does what any sane person would do and immediately buys a new scale.

Weight Gain: Is It Midlife or Menopause?

On average, women put on 5 pounds the first year of menopause, and then 1.5 to 5 pounds per year after age 50. This is unfair and really upsetting. A few extra pounds in a year doesn't seem like a lot, but if you gain 5 pounds a year starting when you are 50, by age 60 you are looking at 50 extra pounds!

In fairness, it's not just menopause that is packing on the pounds. Both men and women gain weight during midlife until it stabilizes around age 60. Even women who continue to menstruate until they are in their late-50s start to gain weight. Clearly there are other factors that have nothing to do with menopause.

Metabolism

I have always told my patients that even if they eat the same and exercise the same as in the 30s, they will gain weight. The mantra has always been that metabolism slows with age, including a change in lean muscle mass, changes in growth hormone, and other factors that are completely out of your control. But a new study released in 2021 established that metabolism doesn't slow down until age 60. Babies, until age 1, have the higher metabolic rate, about 50% higher than adults. From age 1 to about age 20, metabolism gradually slows by about 3 percent a year and then holds steady from age 20 to 60. After age 60, metabolic rate slows, but only by about 0.7 percent a year. More research is needed in this area, but if this is the case, then most midlife weight gain in men and women is due to...

Lifestyle

With the kids finally out of the house, you deserve to dine out and have wine every night, but it does add up. It is also the rare adult who is as physically active in her 50s as when she was in her 20s.

But having said that, it is twice as likely for a midlife woman to be severely obese as a man. Men age. Men have the same lifestyle changes as women. So, what's the difference? The difference is men don't have hot flashes and insomnia. And that's where the menopause factor comes in.

How Hot Flashes Make You Gain Weight

Cortisol

Every time you flash, there is a surge of cortisol. Cortisol, also known as the stress hormone, is produced by the adrenal glands (right above your kidneys). Cortisol has several functions, but one property of cortisol is that it reduces inflammation. When your body is stressed, cortisol increases to reduce inflammation. A small, transient rise in cortisol does not cause problems, but if it is chronically, consistently elevated, there is an increase in blood sugar levels and appetite. The result is that losing weight becomes a losing battle.

Sleep and weight gain
Hot flashes are the number one cause of inadequate sleep during menopause. Seven hours appears to be the magic amount of shut-eye to ensure that the hunger-controlling hormones, leptin, and ghrelin, are at optimal appetite-control levels. Leptin decreases your appetite, and ghrelin increases it. However, ghrelin plays a role in regulating short-term feeding as well as regulates body weight over the long term.

Inadequate sleep translates to low leptin and high ghrelin levels—the exact combo that increases appetite and sabotages your weight loss efforts.

The human sleep cycle is also tied to thyroid function. It appears that inadequate sleep is associated with a lower thyroid-stimulating hormone, which further slows your metabolism.

Inadequate sleep not only slows your metabolic rate, but, if you are exhausted, you will also tend to want pizza instead of grilled veggies. Working out when you are barely functional? Not going to happen.

Given the above, it is not surprising that in SWAN (see chapter 3), the women who gain the most weight during menopause also have the most hot flashes.

What About That Muffin Top?
Any increase in pounds can contribute to that roll that has suddenly emerged from your jeans. But low estrogen also impacts the distribution of weight, even if you haven't gained a pound, so you can totally blame menopause for your new muffin top! Spanx was invented for this reason.

FRANCEY IS NO STRANGER to struggling with her weight. Puberty gifted her 20 pounds and hips she could rest a tray on, and she's tried every fad diet ever since. Vanity aside, Francey realized years ago that, with her family's history, keeping fit is a medical necessity. Overall, between eating carefully and being active, she's usually managed to keep her adult weight within 5 pounds of her college weight. Until now.

The reunion is only two weeks away, but she sets a goal to try to take off enough to zip her dress and then rely on Spanx. But despite a week of no bread (and no martinis), the new scale is stuck. Assuming her thyroid is out of whack, she calls her internist to demand a repeat of the thyroid test that was normal just a few months ago. The repeat thyroid test, shockingly, is completely normal.

You are never going to get your 20-year-old body back, just like you won't regain your wrinkle-free face. But now you understand why you woke up one day and your scale registered your mother's weight. There are ways to get the weight off and keep it from continuing to climb, but this isn't a weight-loss book (check my resources section for some suggestions). So, I am not going to get into the nitty-gritty of how to take off and keep off menopausal weight, beyond making sure that your hot flashes and insomnia are not sabotaging your diet and exercise.

FRANCEY PASSES on the reunion and decides to just focus on work, which has been less than terrific. She is increasingly exhausted from not sleeping most nights. She has even nodded off a few times at her desk. Lately, she can't seem to remember anything, including any of her coworkers' names.

Hot Flashes and Sleep

When hot flashes occur at night, women typically describe them as "night sweats." In one study which used skin conductance monitors to accurately measure the number of flashes, 69% of hot flashes were associated with awakening and accounted for 27% of wakefulness during the night. It is estimated that at least 40% of women lose sleep specifically because of hot flashes. Even if the flashes don't wake you up, women that flash at night have poorer sleep quality and a harder time falling back asleep once they are up.

Beyond making you exhausted and crabby, getting less than 7 hours of sleep per night translates to an increased risk of high blood pressure, diabetes, and heart disease. The news gets even more worrisome for women with diabetes. A 2021 study of over half a million adults with diabetes showed that those who also had insomnia were 87% more likely to die in the following nine years than adults who did not have diabetes or sleep problems.

If you fixed the flashes (or are in the 20% of women who do not flash), you need to figure out other reasons why you are not sleeping. Restless leg syndrome, stress, chronic pain, and sleep apnea are all common causes of insomnia. A snoring bedmate is a whole other problem. A sleep specialist (most large hospitals have one) may be your savior.

Hot Flashes and Cognitive Function

If you can't recall the name of your neighbor's husband, whom you have known for 10 years, you don't need me to tell you that menopause affects your brain. Multiple studies have shown declines in memory and attention, with roughly 44% of perimenopausal women complaining of forgetfulness. A decline in memory was the second-most-frequent complaint in SWAN among perimenopausal women, and studies have confirmed that these memory issues are independent from expected declines due to aging.

In May 2021, the Department of Health and Human Services' Office on Women's Health published a statement citing that up to two-thirds of women in perimenopause report cognitive problems, although estimates as to the extent in affected women differ among experts.

Dr. Pauline Maki, a professor at the University of Illinois at Chicago, is one of the prime researchers in this area. She estimates that 1 in 10 women will have "clinically significant" menopause-related cognitive changes, even into the post-menopause years.

Dr. Maki states,

" Some women experience no symptoms, and others experience clinically meaningful symptoms. The severity and duration of menopause-related declines in memory likely depend on many factors, such as the level of memory skill a woman had before menopause, the severity of sleep and vasomotor symptoms, mood changes, lifestyle factors, a woman's sensitivity to changes in estrogen, and life stressors."

Obviously lack of sleep from hot flashes has an impact on cognitive function. It's impossible to think clearly if you are exhausted. But inadequate sleep aside, menopause has a profound impact on how the brain functions. Neuroimaging studies confirm that women's brains physically change during the menopause transition. There is a loss of both gray matter (brain cells that process information) and white matter (fibers that connect the cells in the gray matter). Memory, word recall, and higher order processing such as creativity, decision making, and reasoning are all affected. Again, though, these changes can be profound for some women and minimal for others.

It's Unclear How Long This Brain Fog Lasts

Some studies report that the brain changes and alteration in cognitive function is exclusively a perimenopause and early post menopause issue, other studies suggest the cognitive issues can linger or be permanent, particularly in women with other risk factors, such as low education, mental health issues, substance use, and a low-income level. It appears that memory and cognition problems are also specifically linked to the number of flashes a woman has, which of course peak during peri and early post menopause. Remember, every time a woman has a hot flash, there is an inflammatory response that causes vascular damage that affects not only the heart but also the brain.

The Alzheimer's connection is also worth noting. One study suggested that women who are at genetic risk for developing Alzheimer's disease later in life first begin to develop amyloid plaques during perimenopause. It has not yet been studied if bothersome hot flashes make those brain changes even worse, but I am betting there is a connection.

Hot Flashes and Quality of Life

Another variable that researchers look at is overall quality of life. Getting to the bottom of it is a lot more scientific than just asking a woman, "How's your life going?" which will likely reflect how her day is going.

Hot flashes and night sweats were shown to be among the top five most bothersome symptoms based on the Menopause-specific Quality of Life Questionnaire (MENQOL). And no surprise, overall, women who flash score lower on MENQOL surveys than women who do not.

And though this book does not go into the details of the impact on your sex life, it goes without saying that cardiovascular disease, insomnia, and pajama-soaking hot flashes are not exactly aphrodisiacs. The typical woman who hasn't had a decent night's sleep in months is not thinking about sex when her head hits the pillow. As expected, there is a high correlation between women who flash and lack of libido.

So whether it is a snoring partner, sleep apnea, restless leg syndrome or hot flashes, sleep is at the top of the list of things that need to be fixed.

FRANCEY'S HOT FLASHES and insomnia are now officially at a crisis level. She hasn't had a decent night's sleep for weeks, and she knows she should get to her gynecologist. But with the time she has already requested to go to the cardiologist and internist, there is no way she can ask for another afternoon off.

After one particularly sleepless night, with flashes every hour on the hour, she falls into a dead sleep at her desk while typing a letter to a donor and wakes up to find she has somehow hit send during her nap.

Just as she starts to panic-read the email in her outbox, which is gibberish, her boss storms over to demand an explanation.

6

HOT FLASHES SHOULDN'T BE WORK

FROM THE C-SUITE to the factory floor, the fatigue, insomnia, anxiety, and impaired memory directly caused by menopause are responsible for women either dropping out of the labor force or underperforming. The devastating impact of hot flashes in the workplace has been well documented but largely ignored, and the time is way overdue to acknowledge and fix it.

Given that flashes typically last an average of seven to 10 years, significant numbers of women, and disproportionately Black women, are dressing for work in layers and hiding a fan under their desk well into their 60s.

The burden personally, but also on work productivity, is dramatic. U.S. studies have documented the decline in learning, memory, and attention during the menopause transition. A 2014 study of over 500,000 women documented that the cost of work lost because of menopause symptoms was $27,668,410 during the 12-month study period. And that did not include the economic impact of additional health care at a price tag of $339,559,458. Yet it is the rare worker who acknowledges that this normal transition that every single woman goes through is responsible for her loss of productivity.

Why the silence? It's not hard to figure out. Beyond the gender bias and ageism that are inherent to the workplace, fear of being ridiculed and becoming the next target of downsizing are both major deterrents to being upfront about the fact that all-day, all-night hot flashes are keeping performance subpar. Many women express concern that if they admit they are struggling, they won't be offered a deserved promotion. And we are not even talking about the fact that it is not unusual for a 48-year-old woman dealing with hot flashes, insomnia, vaginal dryness, painful sex, and recurrent urinary tract infections to report to a 32-year-old male supervisor. Embarrassment and simply wanting to keep things private also contribute to women not speaking up. In one study, only 25% of women felt they could tell their manager the reason for a menopause-related absence.

When I approached HR managers at several companies and offered to give educational talks to women employees about what to expect and how to mitigate symptoms associated with perimenopause and menopause, I was confident that once I pointed out the personal and economic burden to the company, they would enthusiastically bring me in. I had no takers and was told that identifying women over 40 who might be entering menopause would "target them" for discrimination. Better to pretend it wasn't happening.

Interestingly, the attitude regarding menopause in the workplace is very different in the United Kingdom. Most research about the impact of menopause on work has been conducted in the U.K. and paid for by the government.

In a U.K. study of 1,000 working women over the age of 44:

- 77% were having hot flashes.
- 63% felt tired or drowsy while working.
- 47% had trouble concentrating.
- 43% reported memory problems.
- 34% expressed feeling depressed or anxious.
- 41% said they were making more mistakes.
- 43% were losing interest in work.
- 29% had lost confidence in their ability to work effectively.
- 11% declined a promotion.
- 8% consider quitting altogether.

Overall, 63% said that menopause symptoms negatively impacted their work life.

In that same study, 41% directly attributed menopause symptoms to their making mistakes at work, losing confidence, declining a promotion, or even quitting. These cognitive issues are not imaginary.

The U.K. response was swift and commendable. The Government Equalities Office implemented a menopause policy acknowledging that menopause is an occupational health issue and an equality issue. It developed a campaign to spur awareness, education, and guidance as to how best to manage menopause at work, all spelled out on cipd.co.uk/knowledge/culture/well-being/menopause.

There are specific policies in place, including a website dedicated to helping employers develop a menopause policy. The Government Equalities Office even provides posters and leaflets to display at work.

The U.S. should take note. The cost of such programs is minuscule. The savings are potentially in the millions.

Everyday women tell me they need to treat their hot flashes not just because they are miserable, or even out of fear of long-term health problems, but also because they want and need to remain productive. One 40-year-old patient who entered menopause after undergoing chemotherapy took a leave of absence rather than tell her manager what she was going through. Think about that: At the time she needed chemo, she was comfortable sharing that she had cancer and required the treatment to justify time off. But rather than divulge that she was going through a difficult and unexpected transition to menopause, she quit.

It is time to acknowledge that, beyond the impact on personal health and quality of life, menopause is responsible for a huge economic drain on society and on individuals, and it can sabotage a career at the prime of someone's productivity and achievement.

So there you have it: Flashes are far from harmless. Flashes impact on quality of life and the ability to be productive as well as length of life.

THERE IS NO WAY Francey can admit that she is having perimenopausal hot sweats to her boss, who looks like he could be her son, so she makes an excuse about a stomach flu that kept her up all night and promises to do better.

This job is important. She needs to get her brain back in the game. It's time to explore solutions.

Welcome to part 2.

Part 2

MAKE THEM GO AWAY

7

DRESSING IN LAYERS AND OTHER STRATEGIES

A TYPICAL ARTICLE on how to decrease hot flashes (generally written by someone who is decades away from menopause) usually includes helpful suggestions like:

- Dress in layers!
- Turn down the thermostat!
- Avoid spicy foods and red wine!
- Lose some weight!
- Take deep breaths!
- Try hypnosis!
- Acupuncture is awesome!
- Do more yoga!
- Exercise more!
- Buy a fan!

Are they kidding? Are you offended? You should be. And if you had any doubt that the articles were written by someone in their 20s, the overuse of exclamation points is proof positive.

Though dressing in layers and getting a remote control for your thermostat are strategies used by millions, and though it is true that avoiding hot flash triggers such as red wine and spicy food might help, I don't consider those realistic or desirable approaches. I have one patient whose trigger for hot flashes is using her blow-dryer. What is she supposed to do—not dry her hair?

I get it. Many women are highly motivated to put out the fire with behavioral and lifestyle changes. But before investing in a pricey cooling device or signing up for a year's worth of unlimited yoga, it helps to know what works—and what doesn't.

Let's start with the age-old approach of just cooling things down.

Cooling Techniques

Devices to cool down menopausal women are not a new thing.

Getting naked, putting an ice pack under your pillow, wearing "menopause pajamas," and attaching a fan to your headboard all go under this heading. The premise is simple: When you have a hot flash, your core body temperature goes up, the blood vessels in your skin dilate, your skin gets warm, and you sweat. Cooling devices cool you down once the flash has occurred to make you feel more comfortable. Feeling more comfortable is a good thing, but it is not the same as eliminating the flash.

Beyond carrying around a portable fan, there is no shortage of options when it comes to cooling devices. A quick internet search of "menopause cooling products" generates not only hundreds of portable air conditioners, cooling mattresses, vests, and collars, but also a new wave of pricey devices that promise to cool you off 24/7.

One popular device is Meno-Pod™ ($139.99). This small device quickly gets cold so you can discretely place it on your neck to cool down. You can put it in your purse and whip it out when you are feeling the heat. ("Hot flash relief in the palm of your hand!") And not to worry, I'm sure no one will notice when you rummage through your purse and then clamp a white plastic device on the back of your neck while presenting a pitch to a new client.

Another trendy product is Embr Wave™ ($349), a wristband (jewelry!) that claims to be your own personal thermostat. The premise is that it triggers thermal receptors in the body to move heat away from your skin to make you feel cooler and more comfortable. (You can also set it to make you feel warmer if you happen to be cold.) The site clearly states that it will not affect or change your core body temperature, only your perception of the temperature. In a very small, published study (39 women lasting only four weeks), it was shown to help women sleep better. I will admit that wearing a bracelet to cool you down is probably more practical than hauling around a fan and ripping off all your clothes during a board meeting, but personally, I would rather wear David Yurman on my wrist.

AFTER THE MILLIONTH TIME the ad pops up on her Facebook page (how do they know?!), Francey decides to invest in a cooling bracelet. She likes the idea of something that will cool her down more discretely than her desktop fan. It seems to help, but it's not as discrete as she'd hoped. After she's questioned by a third coworker about her new jewelry ("Why would you need a cool-down bracelet?"), she realizes that her new accessory is akin to putting her perimenopause status in the company newsletter—and that is something she isn't ready for.

Given that hot flashes are known to lead to an elevation in cortisol levels, heart rate, and inflammation, which translates to potentially serious medical problems, I personally think it is better to eliminate the hot flash rather than make yourself feel better once it has happened. It's the Band-Aid on the cut as opposed to avoiding the cut in the first place.

Moving on...

For any treatment to be recommended, there are two basic criteria: Is it safe? And does it work? All the listed options are safe. It's the "does it work" criterion that is problematic. Despite enthusiastic testimonials on product websites, many of these interventions have simply not passed the test of being scientifically validated. Even when studies have been done, they are often not reliable for two reasons:

- The number of women in most studies is too small to be valid, and those women often do not have a significant number of hot flashes.
- A placebo effect of a 20% to 50% reduction in the number of hot flashes is typically seen in hot flash trials. The placebo effect is real but lasts only about 12 weeks. Therefore, any trial that runs for three months or less (which includes most trials) does not eliminate the very real, but not sustainable, placebo effect.

Some of the interventions below have been shown to be helpful, but no behavioral or psychological approach has been shown to reduce flashes as much as estrogen therapy. None of these methods are going to eliminate flashes in women whose flashes are severe. But for the woman who is having mild to moderate flashes and wants to avoid pharmaceuticals, there are reasonable options to reduce severity and frequency.

Based on the current published medical literature, here is what is known. As more studies emerge, my conclusions may change.

Cognitive Behavioral Therapy/**Mindfulness**

There are several well-designed scientific studies that support cognitive behavioral therapy (CBT) and mindfulness therapy for the reduction of hot flashes beyond the placebo effect.

CBT and mindfulness training involve learning to recognize and separate thoughts and feelings from physical experiences. They are techniques by which a woman can experience a hot flash but not have an emotional reaction. It's almost like observing someone else having the hot flash instead of experiencing it yourself. Creating psychological distance through mindfulness reduces the negative components of the experience.

In one six-week program of 254 breast cancer survivors who completed a program of internet cognitive behavioral therapy, there was an improvement in hot flashes, night sweats, sleep quality, and overall menopausal symptoms compared to the group that was not enrolled in the program. Those positive results persisted for six months.

Overall, CBT is most helpful when it comes to enhancing sleep and reducing the severity of hot flashes. It is not particularly good at reducing the frequency of hot flashes.

Hypnosis

Hypnosis is a mind-body therapy in which you enter a deeply relaxed state followed by individualized mental imagery and suggestion ("You are in a refrigerator..."). Clinical hypnosis (as opposed to do-it-yourself hypnosis) may be helpful, but the data is not solid. In the most promising study, which included 187 women, the reduction in monitored hot flashes per day was 57% in the hypnosis group compared to the control group. Though favorable, the study was only 12 weeks long—not long enough to account for the placebo effect. So, hypnosis is a potential option, but longer and bigger trials are needed.

Paced Respiration

When you breathe normally, you take about 12 to 14 breaths a minute. By comparison, with paced breathing, you take only five to seven deep diaphragmatic breaths a minute by inhaling through the nose for two to four seconds, and then exhaling through the mouth for four to six seconds. The idea is to focus on your breathing instead of the intensity of the hot flash.

The advantage of paced respiration is that, unlike CBT or mindfulness, this relaxation-based technique is easy to learn and can be self-taught. The downside is that it has never been proven to be helpful in reducing hot flashes.

Weight Loss

There is no question that obesity is associated with more frequent and more severe hot flashes. But, as I pointed out in chapter 5, the mere presence of hot flashes sabotages most weight loss efforts. So, although, theoretically, losing weight will help reduce hot flashes, that's kind of hard to do. One six-month study enrolled obese flashers in an intensive behavioral weight loss intervention. The control group was enrolled in a structured health education program. The weight loss group intervention had a significant improvement in the severity of hot flashes when compared to the control intervention.

Yoga

Yoga goes under the heading of being good for many things (including sleep!), but alleviating menopausal flashes is not one of them. Especially hot yoga.

Iyengar, Indian, yogasana, and Tibetan are among the forms of yoga that have been studied, but in randomized trials, they were not shown to lead to a reduction in the frequency or severity of hot flashes. And it doesn't matter if your yoga practice includes breathing, meditation, poses held for a long time, really expensive yoga clothes, or an extra-long savasana (my favorite part!). Before you write me angry emails that yoga worked for you, I don't doubt it. I am just reporting what the research shows. Although, in complete fairness, wearing fabulous yoga clothes has never adequately been studied.

Exercise

Most studies regarding the impact of exercise on hot flashes have not been well designed and, therefore, are not definitive. Exercise has shown mixed results for reducing hot flashes in symptomatic menopausal women. Like hot yoga, it is no surprise that any activity that increases your core temperature is not going to cool you down.

Interestingly, one well-done study released in 2021 shows that resistance training specifically can reduce hot flashes and night sweats by roughly 50%. The group that stuck to a regimen of three weekly 45-minute sessions with a combination of resistance machines and body weights after four months not only ended up with buff arms but also decreased their hot flash frequency from an average of 7.5 flashes a night to 4.4 flashes over 24 hours. The non-exercisers had no decrease in flashes. So although pumping iron didn't make flashes disappear, there was a significant decrease.

Acupuncture

Acupuncture has been around for over 2,000 years and has proved to be a safe and effective treatment for many medical conditions. No surprise, acupuncture is often cited as an effective treatment to alleviate hot flashes, but like a lot of ancient alternative treatments, it has not consistently been shown to be helpful.

Modern acupuncture often includes modifications, such as manual manipulation, magnets, heat, and ultrasound. Electroacupuncture, one of the newer techniques, utilizes a mild electric current that travels between adjacent needles, resulting in more stimulation than acupuncture using manual techniques.

A 2021 analysis looked at 17 scientifically valid studies involving 1,123 participants that specifically compared acupuncture with nonhormonal prescription drugs that have been shown to reduce hot flashes, such as low-dose antidepressants and gabapentin. (See chapter 10 for more information on nonhormonal prescription options.) Everyone in these studies had a minimum of eight flashes per day, and the studies all utilized placebo acupuncture and placebo drugs. It turns out that the type of acupuncture may be the key. Only electroacupuncture passed the test of being more effective at reducing flashes than placebo pills or sham acupuncture. And though electroacupuncture does not work as well as estrogen, it does appear to work as well as the most commonly prescribed nonhormonal prescription options.

AFTER MENTIONING to her new friend that she is flashing like crazy, Marla assures her that the solution is to do yoga (worked for her!). Seeing as she is not sleeping anyway, Francey signs up for a 6 a.m. class before work.

Little does she know, it is hot yoga. The good news is that no one knows she is sweating from hot flashes. The bad news is that she almost passes out during downward dog.

In summary:

Beneficial Behavioral and Psychological Interventions
- Weight loss.
- Weight training.
- Electroacupuncture.
- Mindfulness.
- CBT.
- Hypnosis.
- Avoidance of food triggers.

Not Proven to be Beneficial Behavioral and Psychological Interventions
- Exercise.
- Yoga.
- Paced Respirations.
- Acupuncture.

AFTER HER VAGINA ISSUES, Francey is totally on board with the idea of drugs, but she is reluctant to make another appointment with Dr. Herpes. She is already on thin ice with her boss after the email debacle, and she is sure the rest of the staff is whispering about her sleepiness, forgetfulness, and general health. If she says she has another doctor's appointment, her boss will probably assume she has some chronic disease that will continue to impact her productivity. If she admits that she is having menopause problems, it will only remind him how old she is.

8

HERBS, BOTANICALS, AND WISHFUL THINKING

"Lydia E. Pinkham's Vegetable Compound will help you."

BACK IN THE 1870s, Lydia Pinkham's Vegetable Compound was a popular cure-all for virtually every gynecologic ailment, including menstrual- and menopause-related problems.

The ads proclaimed Lydia Pinkham's Vegetable Compound to be a "Positive cure for all those painful complaints and weaknesses so common to our best female population and is particularly adapted to the change of life." No doubt, its 13% alcohol content had something to do with its efficacy. Even very proper ladies could remain happily inebriated as they dealt with difficult menopausal symptoms. Another key ingredient of Mrs. Pinkham's remedy (Other than "True and False Unicorn)? None other than black cohosh, an extract of dried roots derived from a plant used by native North American Indians and today one of the most widely used botanical therapies for the treatment of hot flashes.

Lots of herbs have been touted as giving relief for flashes. Unfortunately, most have been shown not to work beyond an initial placebo effect. As discussed in chapter 7, few scientific, well-designed studies on alternative treatments for hot flashes have been completed. These kinds of studies are extremely expensive and difficult to do because a large number of patients and a long time frame are required. In addition, products used in the treatment of hot flashes are particularly tricky to study because the placebo effect is so large. Whether you give women soy, Chinese herbs, or broccoli, at least 30% will experience fewer flashes. Again, the placebo effect is real—it just doesn't last. For about 12 weeks, pretty much any product you believe in will reduce the severity and number of hot flashes and help you sleep. Which would be great...if flashes lasted only 12 weeks.

THAT NIGHT, she consults Dr. Google. (She knows better, but she's desperate.) Her search directs her to the supplement store at the mall, and, after an in-depth consultation with the millennial behind the counter, she spends the proceeds from selling her cooling bracelet on eBay on black cohosh, soy, and red clover. Within one week, she is flash-free. Great success!

Keep in mind that the companies that produce alternatives to estrogen are just as profit motivated as pharmaceutical companies. A multimillion-dollar industry has evolved to promote "natural" products to a vulnerable population of women who are suffering and seeking safe, effective options. Although some women distrust the pharmaceutical industry, which is obligated to test and report all negative findings, the general population seems to have little problem putting its trust in information and promotional ads placed by companies that have no efficacy or safety standards. Just because something is "natural" doesn't mean it is safe. Just because the health food store clerk seems very knowledgeable doesn't mean she knows what works.

There are only two criteria that are appropriate when deciding to use an alternative product: Is it safe? And does it really work? Too often, no one really knows. Because these products are neither foods nor drugs, approval from the Food and Drug Administration is not necessary, and manufacturers are not held responsible for their safety or efficacy. But, fueled by aggressively creative marketing and supported by the placebo effect, along with the fact that, by nature, perimenopausal hot flashes come and go, companies can convincingly market their products with testimonials and "secret proprietary ingredients" that are often the equivalent of oregano. A lucrative industry has evolved, and women spend billions of dollars every year on supplements advertised on the web and recommended by friends or the "expert" at Whole Foods. The only ones who consistently benefit are the companies that sell the products.

It is estimated that between 50% and 75% of postmenopausal women use complementary and alternative therapies for management of menopausal symptoms, and the prevalence may be even higher in breast cancer patients.

The following list is not comprehensive. I have included only the most-purchased botanicals for hot flash relief. The National Institutes of Health has an excellent web-site, https://www.nccih.nih.gov/health/herbsataglance, and is a good source of information to check out other products and to get additional information about herbal supplements.

I have divided the botanicals that claim to decrease hot flashes into the following categories:

Category 1: Shown to be effective
These are products that in large, placebo-controlled trials have scientifically been shown to reduce hot flashes beyond the placebo effect.

Category 2: Shown to be ineffective
These are products that in large, placebo-controlled trials have scientifically been shown to not reduce hot flashes beyond the placebo effect.

Category 3: Possibly effective
These products have conflicting data and may be useful, but more studies are needed.

Category 4: Who knows?
There are no scientific studies published other than in the Journal of Wishful Thinking.

My categories are not based on my opinion; they are based on the scientific studies that are currently available.

I expect there will be readers who will write me angry emails about a product that I listed in category 2, 3, or 4 that worked for them. Unfortunately, anecdotal testimonials are not scientifically valid despite companies using them to sell their products.

It is entirely possible that something I have put in category 2, 3, or 4 may one day be worthy of category 1. But unless you have done a prospective placebo-controlled trial with at least 100 women lasting more than 12 weeks, please do not write to tell me that dong quai completely relieved your hot flashes. I am very happy for you and glad you are no longer suffering, but your anecdotal experience is not a reason for me to recommend it.

Phytoestrogens

What are they?
Isoflavones, also known as phytoestrogens, are nonsteroidal compounds that occur naturally in many plants, fruits, and vegetables. The chemical structure of phytoestrogens is very similar to that of estradiol, so it is not surprising that they have estrogenic properties.

Two types of isoflavones, genistein and daidzein, are found in soybeans, chickpeas, and lentils and are thought to have, of the phytoestrogens, the most potent estrogen-like activity, but still at a much, much weaker rate than human estrogen. Many of the products listed in this chapter are part of the phytoestrogen family.

How well do they work?
The isoflavones have a huge number of studies (we are talking over 15,000!) to determine if they work, but unfortunately, the results are mixed. In a review of 11 randomized clinical trials of soy or isoflavone supplementation, only three of eight trials with at least six weeks of follow-up demonstrated a beneficial effect. In addition, many phytoestrogens have been found to be ineffective. A review of 43 clinical trials found no beneficial effect of phytoestrogens of any type on hot flashes, except for genistein.

Keep in mind there are many isoflavones, in many forms, that are taken in many doses and often together with other herbals. Most studies do not really address safety and efficacy in a useful way. The phytoestrogens, as a group go into Category 3, Possibly effective. There is a wide range of effectiveness depending on the product.

Safety considerations

There are no serious side effects, but many women turn to phytoestrogens because they are trying to avoid estrogen, either because they have breast cancer, or they are under the misconception that estrogen will cause breast cancer. No phytoestrogen has ever been proven to increase the risk of an estrogen positive (ER+) breast cancer recurrence or increase the risk of developing breast cancer, but if you are avoiding estrogen for that reason, you probably should avoid phytoestrogens as well.

Soy and Soy Products

What are they?

Soybeans and other legumes are phytoestrogen plants that contain daidzein. Soy can be eaten as food, but it is also available as a powder in supplement form.

Do they work?

Soy has been shown to reduce cholesterol, lower heart disease rates, and possibly decrease cancer rates. It has also been shown in some, but not all, studies to decrease the number and severity of hot flashes. It turns out that it isn't the daidzein in soy that is the magic ingredient that can provide hot flash relief; it is the *metabolite* of daidzein, known as s-equol. One reason soy study results are mixed is that there is a genetic difference in a woman's ability to metabolize daidzein to s-equol that ultimately determines if ingesting soy or a soy supplement that contains daidzein will be effective.

Two-thirds of North American women are unable to convert daidzein to s-equol and will not get hot flash relief from soy.

One product, S-equol (Equelle™), is sold as the metabolite and avoids that issue. S-equol is the only botanical remedy that the North American Menopause Society recommends. **Category 1: Shown to be effective.**

If soy is your go-to, S-equol is the way to go.

Safety considerations

Soy is part of the phytoestrogen family, with all the same safety considerations. Unless you have a soy allergy, soy in food is not a problem. Some women do experience stomach upset, constipation, or diarrhea. It is also important to note that soy might alter thyroid function if you are deficient in iodine.

Some experts suggest that dietary soy is reasonable in women with ER+ breast cancer but that dietary supplements should be avoided.

Pollen Extract Relizen™

What is it?

One popular product, Relizen™, is made up of pollen and pistils extracted from flowers. Relizen™ claims to reduce menopause symptoms because of its antioxidant and anti-inflammatory properties. It has no estrogenic activity.

Does it work?

Only one small, randomized, controlled study of 53 menopausal women showed significant reductions in vasomotor symptoms on the Menopause Rating Scale (65% versus 38% reported reductions) and in daily diaries (27% showed a greater reduction with treatment) compared to the placebo group. The Menopause Rating Scale also showed significant improvements in other quality-of-life parameters in the pollen extract group

Another small study, which lasted only 12 weeks, reported that hot flashes were reduced by 48.5%, sleep disturbance by 50.1%, depressive mood by 51.2%, irritability by 47.9%, fatigue by 47.8%, vaginal dryness by 39.63%, and muscles and joint pain by 27.4%. Although this is all very encouraging, more studies are needed. **Category 3: Possibly effective.**

Safety considerations
This product is safe, and the manufacturer states there is no pollen in the product, so it is safe for women with pollen allergies.

Hops

What are they?
Yes, these are the same hops used to brew beer! Hop cones are the female (of course!) flower of the hop plant. They have a lovely aroma and are used to add flavors to other grains. The plant contains a phytoestrogen, flavonoid, 8-prenylnaringenin, which has mild estrogenic activity.

Do they work?
This is another one in which evidence is limited and inconsistent. Most research has been done in rats, and though promising, women are not rats. There have been two small human trials using hops to treat symptoms of menopause. Neither showed a positive difference in the

hops group compared to the placebo group. **Category 3: Possibly effective.**

Safety considerations

Assuming you are not drinking barrels of beer to get your hops, there are no major safety concerns beyond the general ones for all phytoestrogens.

Omega-3 Fatty Acids

What are they?

If you eat a lot of fish, you are already getting the known health benefits of omega-3 fatty acids. But in addition to contributing to heart health, lowering your triglycerides, and lowering your blood pressure, manufacturers of omega-3 supplements often claim they reduce flashes.

Do they work?

Another supplement with inconsistent results. In one eight-week (too short!) trial of 91 women randomized to take a placebo or an omega-3 supplement, hot flash frequency and intensity were significantly improved in the omega-3 group. In a 12-week trial, women were randomized to take omega-3s or a placebo and simultaneously do different forms of exercise, such as yoga or aerobic activity. There were no significant differences in hot flashes between the groups. **Category 3: Possibly effective.**

Safety considerations

Omega-3 supplements are safe, unless you count fish breath as a health hazard. There are also reports of upset stomach, diarrhea, and nausea.

Black Cohosh (Remifemin™)

What is it?
When it comes to botanicals and alternative therapies, black cohosh (Actaea racemosa or Cimicifuga racemosa) is one of the most widely used. The active ingredients are unknown, but there is some estrogen-like activity that has been documented.

Does it work?
I really wish I could report otherwise, but despite a handful of individual, small, short-term trials that suggest efficacy, most studies show that black cohosh is no more effective than a placebo. A 2012 review of 16 scientific studies showed no difference between the black cohosh group and the control group as far as hot flash relief. Reluctantly, I am putting it in Category 2: Shown to be ineffective.

Safety considerations
A potential safety concern about black cohosh is its possible estrogenic effect on the breast, but there is no evidence that using it is associated with increased risk of recurrence in women with ER+ breast cancer or uterine cancer. Having said that, some experts suggest that women with breast cancer should avoid its use.

There have also been concerns about possible liver toxicity, but the numbers are low, and although not a huge concern, the possibility is something to be aware of.

Chinese Herbs

What are they?
Chinese herbs might be a combination of any number of herbs, but they also sometimes contain nonherbal

ingredients. I had one patient who had irregular periods, and because of her unexplained, sky-high estrogen levels, I was concerned that she had an estrogen-producing ovarian tumor. When I asked her about medications, she reported only that she was taking Chinese herbs to help her sleep. I looked at the bottle, but it was in a language that I don't speak. I convinced her to stop taking her "herbs," and her estrogen level dropped to normal levels within a week.

Do they work?
A 2016 review analyzed data from 63 studies and found that Chinese herbal therapy is ineffective for the treatment of menopausal hot flashes. Many Chinese herbs are combinations of multiple herbs, which makes them particularly difficult to study when it comes to efficacy and safety. **Category 2: Shown to be ineffective.**

Safety considerations
According to the National Institutes of Health: "Some Chinese herbal products have been contaminated with toxic compounds, heavy metals, pesticides, and microorganisms and may have serious side effects. Manufacturing errors, in which one herb is mistakenly replaced with another, also have resulted in serious complications."

Crinums (Crila™)

What are they?
Crinums are members of the amaryllis family and are primarily used in South Asia. Extracts are said to exert anti-tumor, immune-modulating, analgesic, and antimicrobial properties. Crila™ will put a $139 dent in your bank account to "promote uterine health and defend against hot flashes." And, good news, you can share the bottle with the

man in your life because the same product (with a different label) claims to "maintain prostate health" and lead to "better bladder emptying."

Do they work?
There are no studies in the scientific literature (unless you count a 2005 study published in Vietnam that basically says men liked it). All reports of efficacy are anecdotal. A firm **Category 4: Who knows?**

Safety considerations
Who knows?

Dong Quai

What is it?
Dong quai, also known as Angelica sinensis, is a plant with lovely little white flowers. It has been used in traditional Chinese medicine as the go-to herb for pretty much every gynecologic problem, including, you guessed it, hot flashes. It has been shown to have estrogen-like activities in female rats but not female humans.

Does it work?
In 10 clinical trials, no reduction in the frequency of flashes was seen with dong quai. Critics of these trials say that the doses were too low and that, to be effective, dong quai needs to be mixed with other botanicals. **Category 2: Shown to be ineffective.**

Safety considerations
Unlike most herbals, which are pretty benign, this one scares me. Dong quai has been shown to cause rats to have uterine bleeding. I know, humans are not rats...but still. It

is potentially carcinogenic and has been shown to cause anticoagulation and photosensitivity. So even if it did work, which it doesn't, I would not recommend it.

Evening Primrose Oil

What is it?

Evening primrose, Oenothera biennis L, is a flowering plant rich in linolenic acid. Oil from evening primrose seeds is used in a variety of soaps and cosmetics. And aside from hot flashes, it is claimed to treat a variety of inflammatory and autoimmune disorders, including irritable bowel syndrome, eczema, and arthritis.

Does it work?

There was only one randomized trial that compared evening primrose oil to a placebo. Of 35 women, half received evening primrose oil, and half received plain oil. The good news is that the women who took evening primrose oil all experienced a reduction in their hot flashes. The bad news is, so did the women in the placebo group. There was zero difference between the two groups. In all fairness, this trial was too small and too short to draw any conclusions, which throws evening primrose oil into **Category 4: Who knows?**

Safety considerations

Possible side effects include nausea, diarrhea, upset stomach, and headache in some people. There are some reports of estrogen-like activity, so those trying to avoid that should not take it.

Flaxseeds

What are they?
Flaxseeds or linseeds (Linum usitatissimum) are a popular phytoestrogen and a rich source of lignans. The lignans in flaxseeds reside in cell walls and are not bioavailable without extensive crushing. So if you decide to swallow flaxseeds, you need to crush them first. Flaxseed oil is not the same thing.

Do they work?
Flaxseeds were not shown to be more effective than a placebo for hot flashes in two randomized, placebo-controlled, double-blind trials. To date, the accumulated evidence for flaxseeds in a review of five studies does not support its use. **Category 2: Shown to be ineffective.**

Safety considerations
Flaxseed meal, flour, and oil are safe as foods. Bloating and mild diarrhea have been reported in women who use flaxseeds regularly. And there are all the same concerns as with other phytoestrogens.

Maca

What is it?
Maca is a root grown exclusively in the Peruvian Andes. It is generally found in powder or liquid form as a supplement, but it is also a food. Some people put it in their smoothies. It's loaded with carbs and relatively high in calories (for those who care). It is sometimes referred to as Peruvian ginseng. Maca contains a weak phytosterol. In the laboratory, some estrogenic activity has been demonstrated, but that has not been duplicated in humans. It is said to

increase strength and stamina, athletic performance, and male fertility, as well to serve as an aphrodisiac and to relieve hot flashes.

Does it work?

Hard to say. There are currently four published studies that show a reduction in flashes, but the studies are small and poorly designed. **Category 3: Possibly effective.**

Safety considerations

Maca is generally considered to be safe. However, if you have thyroid problems, you may want to avoid it because it contains goitrogens, a substance known to interfere with thyroid function.

Pine Bark **Pycnogenol™**

What is it?

Proanthocyanidins derived from pine bark are promoted as an antioxidant and sold under the registered trademark Pycnogenol™. This compound is also found in grape seeds. It has been used for years to help with asthma as well as eye damage in diabetics. It is also promoted for hot flash relief.

Does it work?

One frequently quoted study involved only 70 women who took Pycnogenol™ for eight weeks and reported a decrease in every single menopause symptom, including hot flashes. Aside from being too short and too small of a study, there was no control group. In other words, the results are meaningless. Three other trials for "menopausal symptoms" are published, but there is no specific data on hot flashes, winning Pycnogenol™ a coveted spot in Category 4: Who knows?

Safety considerations
Dizziness and upset stomach have been reported. (It's tree bark!)

Red Clover

What is it?
Red clover is an herb that grows wild in meadows in Europe, Asia, and recently North America. It is loaded with the phytoestrogens genistein and daidzein. It is often ingested as a tea.

Does it work?
Red clover is all over the map with mixed results. A 2015 review article looked at 183 publications on red clover and hot flashes. Only 11 studies met the criteria to ensure scientific reliability, and, in those studies, red clover was shown to be ineffective for hot flashes. In the other studies, although some criteria were met, they were still felt to be too inadequate to make a real determination. **Category 3: Possibly effective.**

Safety considerations
Same as the other phytoestrogens. Red clover may enhance the effect of blood-thinning drugs, increasing the risk of bleeding. Headache, rashes, and nausea have been reported. However, animals, specifically sheep, that graze on large amounts of red clover have become temporarily or permanently infertile. (I know, women are not sheep.)

Wild Yam

What is it?

Mexican yams, also known as wild yam root, contain diosgenin, a steroid building block that has estrogen-like activity. This extract is often put in the form of a capsule to swallow or a cream to be applied to the skin. Diosgenin is a phytoestrogen that can be chemically converted into progesterone. But this is important: Wild yams do not contain progesterone. And, furthermore, the body cannot change diosgenin into progesterone; that can be done only in a lab.

Does it work?

Despite claims that wild yam root will treat all your menopausal symptoms and prevent or treat osteoporosis, there is no scientific evidence that is the case. A small study published in 2001 included 23 women who applied the cream for three months. Nothing bad happened, but nothing good happened either. Although wild yam cream is often advertised as a "natural estrogen" or "natural progesterone," it is not one. So, all those yam creams that claim to increase your hormone levels? That is not biologically possible. **Category 2: Shown to be ineffective.**

Safety considerations

Many creams that claim to have yam extract do not contain any. Others are infiltrated with undisclosed hormones, including estrogen and progesterone. Wild yam applied to the skin, however, does not appear to have any serious side effects.

And for those of you who, after reading this chapter, think I have something against herbs, I think you will like the chapter on cannabis.

WHEN A CANNABIS DISPENSARY opens down the block, Francey and Marla head over to see if it has something that can help with flashes and insomnia. Although Francey smoked her fair share of weed in college, that was for fun. Now she is on a mission. She has no clue what to buy, so she corners the oldest-looking employee she can find (who looks around 16) and asks for advice. After a quick lecture on terpenes, THC, and CBD (huh?), the salesperson hands her a box of raspberry gummies and says, "Trust me." The last time someone said "trust me" was her ex as he was leaving on a business trip. He came home with a girlfriend, who is now his wife.

Despite her misgivings, she decides to give the gummies a try, mostly because they look delicious.

9

CAN CANNABIS COOL YOU DOWN?

IT'S NOT NEWS that Americans turn to cannabinoids for pretty much everything that ails them. So it is no surprise that in a 2020 study, 27% of menopausal women reported that they used some form of pot to alleviate hot flashes, insomnia, vaginal dryness, mood swings, and brain fog. That's more than 1 in 4 women—and the numbers are probably now much higher. Compare that to the mere 7% of women who take systemic estrogen to alleviate symptoms.

Women are smoking pot, drinking it, and infusing it in oil and putting it not only on their avocado toast but also on their vulva and in their vagina.

Cannabis to Treat Menopausal Symptoms Is Not a New Thing

According to historian Ethan Russ, cannabis (the scientific name of the marijuana plant) was used as far back as the 7th century for myriad women's ailments. In 1889, cannabis suppositories were used during menopause to treat *"the well-known symptoms, the various reflexes, the excitement, the irritability, and pain in the neck or the bladder, flashes of heat and cold, [and] according to my experience, can frequently be much mitigated, by the suppositories."*

Cannabis indica even pops up as a treatment of menopause in the 1899 edition of the Merck Manual, a popular medical textbook. The manual also recommends a "change of air and scene."

Climacteric Disorders.—*See also, Metrorrhagia.*

Acid, Hydriodic.
Aconite: 1 minim hourly for nervous palpitations and fidgets.
Ammonia: as inhalation. Raspail's Eau Sédative locally in headache: take Sodii chloridum, Liq. ammoniæ, each 2 fl. oz.; Spiritus camphoræ; 3 fl. drs.; Aqua to make 2 pints.
Ammonium Chloride: locally in headache.
Amyl Nitrite.
Belladonna.
Calabar Bean: in flatulence, vertigo, etc.
Camphor: for drowsiness and headache.
Cannabis Indica.
Change: of air and scene useful adjunct.
Cimicifuga: for headache.
Eucalyptol: flushings, flatulence, etc.
Hot Spongings.

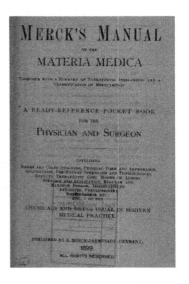

I love the notion that women suffering from hot flashes and insomnia were advised by their physician to smoke pot and take a vacation.

At the turn of the century, all the major pharmaceutical companies, Eli Lilly, Parke-Davis (now Pfizer), and Squibb, sold cannabis as a powder, tablet, and tincture.

Does It Work?

Other than wildly enthusiastic anecdotal reports, there have been inadequate scientific studies in large groups of women over an extended period of time with a control group using fake pot as a comparison. In other words, the kinds of studies that are required for pharmaceutical agents to become FDA-approved don't exist when it comes to cannabinoids. In addition, most studies on the effect of cannabinoids include only men—and women are not little men (or rats).

Aside from being expensive, studies on the impact of cannabis on menopause symptoms would be difficult to conduct. The pharmacology is complex. There are well over 100 cannabinoids, and all have different physical and psychological effects. The dosage and type of cannabis are difficult to standardize and are also dramatically altered by variables, such as other medications someone might be taking.

Don't get me wrong: I think the use of cannabinoids to relieve menopause symptoms is very promising, and, based on the known properties of cannabinoids, there is good reason that they would be beneficial in alleviating many symptoms of menopause. It just would be nice to have more research that informs me as to what kind of cannabis and what dosage works best so that I can make informed recommendations to my patients. But, having said that, here is what is known based on the science of cannabinoids and observational, anecdotal data.

Our Personal Endocannabinoid System

Believe it or not, the human body makes its own cannabinoids. The human endocannabinoid system is a complex nerve-signaling system composed of neurotransmitters that bind to cannabinoid receptors. It is responsible for regulating multiple body functions, including appetite, metabolism, pain, mood, learning, memory, sleep, stress, bone health, and cardiovascular health—pretty much everything that keeps humans functional and balanced.

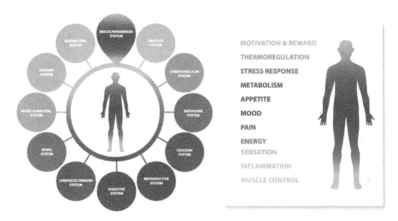

There are three components to the endocannabinoid system.

- **Endocannabinoids** are made in the body. The two main endocannabinoids that have been studied are:
  - anandamide (AEA).
  - 2-arachidonoylglyerol (2-AG).
- Equally important are the **endocannabinoid receptors**, which are required for endocannabinoids to become active.
  - **CB1 receptors** are mostly found in the central nervous system (brain and spinal cord) but also the reproductive system, heart, lungs, skin, and adrenal glands.
  - **CB2 receptors** are found in the liver, bones, spleen, digestive tract, peripheral nervous system, and immune system.

- The third component of the endocannabinoid system are **enzymes**, which break down the endocannabinoids after they have done their job.
  - Fatty acid amide hydrolase (FAAH) breaks down AEA.
  - Monoacylglycerol lipase (MAGL) breaks down 2-AG.

In addition to doing good things, such as regulating appetite, mood, motivation, and pleasure, one of the primary endocannabinoids, anandamide, also helps regulate body temperature.

(You know where I'm going here.)

Endocannabinoids and Estrogen

It turns out that hormones, specifically estrogen, play a critical role in the endocannabinoid system. Estrogen regulates fatty acid amide hydrolase (FAAH), the enzyme that breaks down anandamide.

Some experts propose that the disruption in the endocannabinoid system when estrogen is low is responsible for menopause symptoms and is also why using cannabis decreases hot flashes. Possible benefits to using cannabis for menopause symptom relief beyond reducing hot flashes include:

- Sleep.
- Sexual function (libido, lubrication, orgasm).
- Anxiety reduction.
- Bone metabolism (helps build bone!).
- Pain reduction (which also helps with sleep).

Phytocannabinoids 101

Phytocannabinoids are extracted from the marijuana plant, aka cannabis.

Since 2021, the legalization of cannabis has swept the country, and chances are good that you either live in a state or are a quick drive away from a state that has no shortage of dispensaries. In a 2020 Gallup poll, 68% of the U.S. population supported the legalization of recreational marijuana. The reason for this overwhelming support is that cannabis is more than just a pretty plant. Aside from the "this makes me feel really good" part, the medicinal value cannot be ignored.

The two cannabinoids extracted from the cannabis flower that have potential roles in managing menopause symptoms are tetrahydrocannabinol (THC) and cannabidiol (CBD). And, no surprise, only the female flower contains these elements.

Tetrahydrocannabinol (THC)

THC is the psychoactive component of cannabis. It activates CB1 receptors and can create a euphoric feeling.

THC mimics some aspects of anandamide, the endocannabinoid that helps regulate body temperature, which is theoretically why THC is the key to reducing hot flashes.

Cannabidiol (CBD)

CBD is extracted from hemp flowers. It does not have psychoactive properties, so it will not get you high. CBD contains trace amounts of THC. Although CBD may not reduce hot flashes specifically, it does decrease pain and inflammation, in addition to helping you get a good night's sleep.

The anti-inflammatory properties of both cannabinoids also may help with bone loss and cardiovascular disease.

Kinds of Cannabis Plants

Indica: This species of cannabis comes from a short, bushy plant and is anecdotally known for its calming attributes. Indica is used for pain relief, sleep, and relaxation, and it is best taken at night.

Sativa: The sativa species is a tall, slim plant and is often used during the day because it is purported to boost energy, increase focus, and be overall stimulating instead of sedating.

Hybrid: A hybrid plant has aspects of indica and sativa, mixing their effects to get the best of both strains. The interbreeding of these hybrid strains has become so common that some say the unique distinctions between indica and sativa no longer exist. There are many variables that determine what you are getting. Levels of THC and CBD in these different species are all over the map.

Strains vary depending on the grower, geographic location, the nutrients used, even the schedule of lighting. If you buy the same strain in Colorado that you bought in Oregon, it may not make you feel the same. All cannabis brands are not equal, and each product will affect you differently. In other words, once you find a brand you like and trust, stick with it.

Getting It Where It Needs to Go

Eat it? Smoke it? Rub it on? So many choices. Personally, I think chocolate infused with CBD is an excellent choice, but this is not a scientific conclusion. I just like chocolate. But seriously, *very seriously,* how you take your cannabis is important—not only in terms of what it will do for you, but also in terms of onset of action and potential side effects. The onset of action, peak levels, and total duration of effect listed here are very approximate and unreliable, but I have included them just to give you an idea.

Smoking or vaping

Inhaling your cannabis has the advantage of an immediate effect, but the disadvantage is potentially harming your respiratory tract. It also has the disadvantage of not being an activity you can do discretely. Smoking a joint may not be something you want to do at work or while having dinner with your in-laws. And though your teenage kids will be delighted that their mom is smoking weed, you may not want the telltale aroma wafting through your house. The experience is variable depending on the number and spacing of puffs as well as the hold time and how deeply and how much you inhale.

Onset of action: Within minutes.

Peak levels: About 15 to 30 minutes.

Total duration: About two or more hours.

Edibles

Edibles include foods infused with cannabis. They are usually delicious foods, such as gummies, chocolate, ice cream, smoothies, cookies—the possibilities are endless. The effect is delayed, which sometimes leads to overdosing (more on this later). There would probably be a lot less overdosing if the cannabis were infused in brussels sprouts instead of brownies. Edibles are not psychoactive unless they contain more than trace amounts of THC.

Onset of action: 30 to 90 minutes.

Peak levels: Two to six hours.

Total duration: At least four to eight hours.

Sublinguals

Sublinguals are tinctures, sprays, or strips placed under the tongue that are quickly absorbed into the bloodstream through a plexus of blood vessels. They are different from edibles in that they do not make the trip through the digestive system but, rather, are absorbed directly into the bloodstream. It is important to not eat or drink immediately after using a sublingual, and make sure that it stays under the tongue. The advantage is a relatively quick onset of action along with bypassing the gut and the lungs. Also, it appears that THC is absorbed better as a sublingual than as an edible. Some edibles (chocolate, ice cream) can be placed under the tongue and allowed to melt.

Onset of action: About 15 to 30 minutes.
Peak levels: Around 45 minutes.
Total duration: One to four hours.

Topicals

Topicals include any cannabis-infused products applied to the skin, including lotions, patches, oils, sprays, and soaps. Absorption is slow, and the effects are primarily at the location where they are applied, which is why topicals are typically used to alleviate pain in a specific area of the body.

Onset of action: Within minutes.

Peak levels: About 10 minutes.

Total duration: Hours or even days (highly variable).

While we are on the subject of topical applications, CBD oil applied directly to the vulva, vagina, or clitoris may be useful as a lubricant or to increase blood flow, which in turn may help with sexual function and orgasm. The details are in *Slip Sliding Away: Turning Back the Clock on Your Vagina* and *Put the O Back into Mojo: A Post Menopause Guide to Orgasm.*

Hot Flash **Relief?**

So here we go. This has not been scientifically studied, so what I am going to say is based on the known pharmacology of cannabinoids and anecdotal information from folks in this world. But, yes, it does appear that cannabis is effective in decreasing the frequency and severity of hot flashes.

Again, the THC in cannabis mimics anandamide, the endocannabinoid that helps regulate body temperature. This effect when using cannabis is dose dependent. Large amounts of THC cause your internal temperature to drop, while small amounts can cause your internal temperature to rise. In other words, THC can regulate your internal thermostat, but it is important to use the right amount.

How Much **Should You Take?**

I will give you some general dosing guidelines, but they are not based on scientific studies. I'm just telling you what I have been told. The dosage is a free-for-all, and even the pharmacists who work in the industry and appear very knowledgeable are basing their recommendations on anecdotal reports and individual experience as opposed to scientific studies. Remember, most of the folks who work in dispensaries are not medical practitioners, but they often give medical recommendations. They may not be aware of a potential drug interaction or other medical variables.

Effects are dependent on:

- Age.
- Dose.
- Route.
- Potency.
- Tolerance.
- Medications.
- Genetic factors.
- Hormonal status.
- Time of last meal.
- Alcohol consumption.
- Frequency of consumption.
- Other additives in the product.

All those variables are important, but the number one thing that impacts on dosing is your sex. Let's start with the known fact that young women metabolize cannabis more slowly than men and...

Women post-menopause metabolize cannabis more slowly than women pre-menopause.

This makes sense given that cannabis metabolism is facilitated by estrogen, and post-menopause, women don't have any. Edibles are particularly problematic. As a sweeping generalization, menopausal women tend to prefer to eat a cookie rather than smoke a joint—and menopausal women tend to eat the WHOLE cookie. There is a delayed onset of action, and it can take up to two hours to metabolize. Many women, thinking that the cookie is not working, eat another cookie and overdose, leading not only to feeling stoned, but sometimes also to feeling disoriented and frightened. Edibles are frequently sold at an individual serving of 10 mg of THC, which is way more than most menopausal women should be ingesting! If you are going the edible route, start with a low dose and wait *at least* 90 minutes before deciding it isn't working and taking more.

General Dosage Guidelines **for Hot Flash Relief**
There is no one-size-fits-all dosing, and because cannabis is a botanical, you cannot count on the same level of consistency as you would with a commercial pharmaceutical. Keeping a journal is a good idea until you figure out what works best for you.

Having said that and understanding that I have no studies to rely on, here are guidelines for hot flash relief supplied by Luba Andrus, RPH, BS, MJ, a cannabis pharmacologist I consulted who routinely works with menopausal women.

Guidelines for THC
1. Sublingual is preferred.
2. Start at 1.25 mg once or twice daily.
3. Titrate up every five to seven days.
4. 2 mg to 4 mg works for most women.

Guidelines for CBD
1. Sublingual is preferred.
2. Use an indica-dominant product.
3. Start at 2.5 mg twice daily.
4. Titrate up every four to seven days.
5. Continue until 20 mg is reached.
6. Keep in mind that it can take upwards of 30 days to feel the full effect, so be patient.

Guidelines for THC/CBD-Combined Products
1. Sublingual is preferred.
2. CBD/THC ratio should be 20:1 or higher.
3. 22% to 26% THC and 0.76% CBD is a common combo.
4. Products with a high THC:CBD ratio are best taken in the evening or at bedtime.

Estrogen and the Entourage Effect
So, what's better: estrogen or pot? In the absence of studies, estrogen remains the gold standard. But instead of picking estrogen *or* cannabis, there is a case to be made for using both together. This is because of a concept known as the entourage effect.

It appears that the different compounds found in the cannabis plant work synergistically to produce a greater effect than if taken separately. Some experts believe that using cannabinoids along with estrogen enhances this entourage effect. In other words, using estrogen and cannabinoids together will work better than using either one alone.

One obvious question is, if you are already using cannabis and then start taking estrogen, will it change the way the cannabis makes you feel or the dose you should be taking? I have no idea. Yet another area where more research is desperately needed.

Summing It **All Up**
- Although there is a scarcity of scientific studies to back it up, cannabis appear to decrease the frequency and severity of hot flashes.
- **THC** is likely the component that is most important for **hot flash relief** because it mimics some aspects of anandamide, the endocannabinoid naturally occurring in the body that helps regulate body temperature.
- **CBD** decreases pain and inflammation in addition to helping you get a **good night's sleep**.
- A **product with both CBD and THC** is probably best for hot flash relief but finding the right dose may require some trial and error.
- Small, spaced-out doses (micro-dosing) is best.
- A sublingual product has a fast onset and avoids the gastrointestinal system and the respiratory system. The THC in such products is absorbed the best, and it is controllable, with more predictable dosing. Bonus: There are no calories unless it is a product that is flavored with sugar and syrups.

CAUTION!
- Cannabinoids have the **potential to interact with certain medicines, such as blood thinners and antiseizure drugs**. In some cases, they can potentially make other medications less effective.
- Cannabis is generally felt to be safe, but the side effects may include brain fog, dry mouth, unsteady gait, diarrhea, and drowsiness.

- A glass of water at the bedside is a good idea since you may wake up in the middle of the night and be thirsty.
- Cannabis users need up to twice the sedation for medical procedures. If you partake, be sure to tell your anesthesiologist! (You *do* want to get the right amount of anesthesia.)
- The effects of cannabinoids are dose related. Low to moderate doses appear to have positive effects on sexual function and responsiveness (loss of inhibition, increased sensitivity). High doses can be a problem and are associated with an increase in paranoia and anxiety. There is such a thing as too much of a good thing.
- Again, menopausal women are more vulnerable than men to an overdose: The estrogen connection is likely the reason women metabolize cannabinoids differently than men (beyond having a lower body weight), and post-menopause women metabolize cannabinoids very slowly.

When it comes to edibles, "go low and start slow."

THAT NIGHT, FRANCEY POPS *a gummy, but an hour later, she is still wide awake and flashing, so she pops another two, just to be sure. She finally drifts off and wakes up to realize she has been sleeping for 12 hours, she feels foggier than ever, her mouth is drier than her vagina ever was, and she is now late for work. Despite Googling on her lunch hour, she can't find any consistent, credible information on exactly what kind of cannabis will help hot flashes or how best to take it. Deciding that she is not up for being her own experiment, she goes home and flushes the rest of her gummies down the toilet.*

Dr. Streicher's Survey **on Cannabis and Menopause Symptoms**

Many of you reading this book may have participated in research I am conducting about the use of cannabis for relief of menopause symptoms. Thank you for taking the time to fill out the survey!

The results have not been published in a medical journal (yet!), but here are preliminary statistics from hundreds of women who use cannabis to relieve hot flashes, or insomnia.

Who Advised You What to Buy?

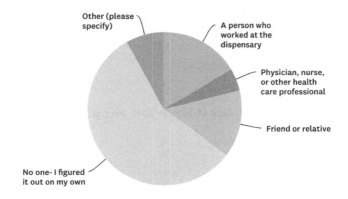

How Do You Consume Cannabis?

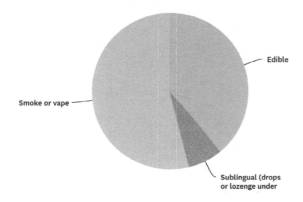

Does It Help Reduce the Number or Severity of Your Hot Flashes?

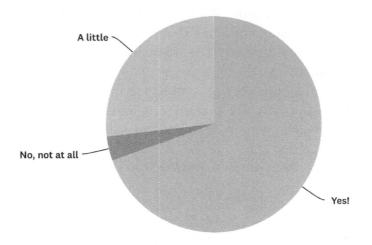

Does it Help You Sleep?

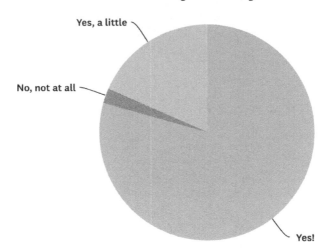

*Full disclosure: I wrote this chapter while spending a few days on **Jim Belushi's Farm**, meeting with cannabis experts and chocolatiers who infuse their sweets with CBD.

Courtesy of Glacier™ chocolates

Courtesy of Bhang™ chocolates

The cute guy in the gray shirt is my husband, Jason.

IT'S NOT AS IF SHE WERE THE FIRST WOMAN to have hot flashes, for god's sake. Francey already knows that her mom was a flasher too. So when her mom returns from her bike trip through Madagascar (82 and with more energy than Francey!), she asks her how she managed her menopause (Francey has never asked her mom about vaginal dryness and doesn't really want to visualize her mom having sex).

Mom tells her that Premarin™ was a godsend, a life-changer, and her answer to a decent night's sleep. She happily took her estrogen pill until that big study came out that scared the hell out of everyone and her doctor advised her to stop.

Putting a little estrogen on her vagina is one thing, but taking it systemically makes Francey more than a little nervous, especially after reading warnings about cancer, blood clots and dementia, so she decides to learn about non-hormonal options before jumping on the estrogen bandwagon.

10

A TRIP TO THE PHARMACY FOR A NON-ESTROGEN RX

AFTER SPENDING A MONTH'S SALARY on all manner of herbs, spices, and products recommended by the experts at Whole Foods and still waking up every hour on the hour, you may want to think about going the prescription route. I am aware that despite the reassurances of menopause experts like myself, most women choose to avoid estrogen, or have been advised by their doctors to steer clear, but fortunately there are several nonhormonal prescription medications to douse the fire.

None of the drugs listed in this chapter work as well as estrogen at reducing the frequency of flashes, but some of these nonhormonal options do a reasonably good job of turning severe flashes into more manageable mild or moderate flashes. This is particularly important for women with breast cancer, who do not have the option of estrogen therapy.

Interestingly, none of these drugs, other than Brisdelle™ (Paroxitene 7.5 mg), were developed with the intention of treating hot flashes but were serendipitously found to help when they were being used to treat other conditions. Brisdelle™ is, at this time, the only nonhormonal drug that is FDA approved for the treatment of hot flashes. All the other medications listed that are frequently used to treat hot flashes go under the heading of "off label" use.

"Off Label" Doesn't Mean "Off Limits"

Prescribing drugs for a different condition or for a different population than the U.S. Food and Drug Administration (FDA) originally intended and approved is known as off-label prescribing, and it's something every doctor does. When a drug is prescribed off label, it doesn't mean that the drug is illegal or that it won't work, but simply that it is being used to treat something other than what it was developed and originally intended for. Hundreds of drugs are prescribed off label. As an example, every birth control pill on the market has been FDA-approved to prevent pregnancy. But 30% of birth controls are legitimately prescribed for reducing menstrual cramps, treating endometriosis, or decreasing heavy bleeding, all off-label reasons.

Selective serotonin reuptake inhibitors, also known as SSRIs, are intended and FDA approved to be used as antidepressants, but they were serendipitously found to significantly reduce hot flashes in menopausal women. For years my go-to alternative to estrogen therapy has been to prescribe off label an SSRI such as paroxetine or a serotonin or a norepinephrine reuptake inhibitor (SNRI) such as venlafaxine.

The Specifics on Nonhormonal Medications Commonly Used to Treat Hot Flashes

I am intentionally not giving recommended doses for most of the following drugs. This is not a do-it-yourself project. Dosing must be individualized, and many factors must be considered. In addition, some of these drugs need to be started at a low dose and gradually increased if tolerated to get to a dose that works.

Paroxetine mesylate 7.5 mg (Brisdelle™)

What is it?
It's an SSRI that is the only nonhormonal drug FDA approved for the treatment of moderate to severe hot flashes. *Because it is a lower dose than the SSRIs used to treat depression, it does not have negative side effects such as weight gain and sexual problems.*

The good news
- Reduces frequency of flashes 25% to 69%.
- Reduces the severity of flashes more than the frequency.
- Decreases the number of night awakenings.
- No impact on weight.
- No impact on libido or orgasm.
- Unlike the higher-dose SSRIs, it does not need to be tapered when stopping treatment.

Cautions, side effects, and downsides
- Not always covered by insurance.
- Many experts advise avoiding SSRIs in women taking tamoxifen because all SSRIs may theoretically block the conversion of tamoxifen to its active form. This is controversial because it has not been proven.
- The 7.5 mg dose cannot, and should not, be prescribed for the treatment of depression. It will not work.
- Side effects are infrequent but include nausea, vomiting, drowsiness, dizziness, trouble sleeping, and loss of appetite.

Selective Serotonin Reuptake Inhibitors (SSRIs)
Paroxetine hydrochloride (Paxil™, Pexeva™), citalopram (Celexa™), escitalopram (Lexipro™)

What are they?
Paroxetine, citalopram, and escitalopram are SSRIs FDA approved for the treatment of major depressive disorder, obsessive-compulsive disorder, panic disorder, and generalized anxiety disorder.

The good news
- Reduce flashes 25% to 69%.
- Reduce severity more than frequency.
- SSRIs work fast in terms of treating flashes. Unlike when these drugs are used to treat depression, the effect is usually noticed in days as opposed to weeks.
- Women taking an SSRI for the treatment of depression will also get the hot flash benefit.
- Available as generics.

Cautions, side effects and downsides
- Decrease libido and the ability to orgasm in up to 30% of women.
- Up to 25% of women gain weight.
- Many experts advise avoiding SSRIs in women who are taking tamoxifen because all SSRIs may theoretically block the conversion of tamoxifen to its active form. This is controversial because it has not been proven.
- Sertraline and fluoxetine are SSRIs that have NOT been shown to have a significant effect on hot flashes.
- When discontinuing, SSRIs should be tapered, especially if being given at a higher dose.

A logical question is, why bother with a lower, 7.5 mg dose that may not be covered by insurance? Why not just use paroxetine in the available 10 mg or higher doses that are used to treat major depressive disorder, obsessive-compulsive disorder, panic disorder, and generalized anxiety disorder? Why not just cut a generic paroxetine 10 mg pill in half?

- The 10 mg dose of generic paroxetine available for the treatment of depression is 33% higher than needed to relieve hot flashes.
- Many women do not want to take an antidepression drug when they are not depressed, just hot.
- Higher doses of paroxetine need to be tapered when the drug is discontinued.
- In clinical trials, 5 mg did not give hot flash relief, so cutting your 10 mg pill in half won't cut it.
- *And the most important reason: The side effects seen in higher doses of paroxetine, primarily sexual problems, and weight gain, are not seen at the 7.5 mg dose.*

Gabapentin
FusePaq™, Fanatrex™, Gabarone™, Gralise™, Neurontin™

What is it?
- Gabapentin is an anti-epileptic drug FDA approved for the treatment of a variety of conditions, including partial seizures, post-herpetic nerve pain, shingles, and diabetes.

The good news

- Works particularly well for women who flash at night because of its sedative effect and its ability to reduce hot flashes in the first four hours of sleep.
- In some studies, works as well as estrogen, but only in high doses that are usually not tolerated.
- If night sweats do occur, many women find that they fall back asleep more easily than they did pretreatment.
- Available as a generic.

Cautions, side effects, and downsides

- Side effects include headache, dizziness, lethargy, sleepiness, impaired balance, and disorientation (nighttime dosing is best).
- Most women prefer taking an SSRI or SNRI when compared to gabapentin by a 2-to-1 ratio.
- Has an FDA warning regarding uncommon suicidal thoughts.
- Must start at a low dose and titrate up.

Serotonin-Norepinephrine Reuptake Inhibitors (SNRIs) Venlafaxine (Effexor™), desvenlafaxine (Pristiq™, Khedezla™)

What are they?

Venlafaxine and desvenlafaxine are SNRIs FDA approved for the treatment of depression.

The good news

- Reduction in frequency of hot flashes varies from 25% to 69%, with improvements in severity from 27% to 61%.

- As with SSRIs, the clinical response is more rapid (days) than the typical response to SNRIs for depression (weeks).
- Can be used by women taking tamoxifen.

Cautions, side effects, and downsides
- May cause nausea and vomiting.
- When discontinuing, should be tapered to avoid withdrawal symptoms.

Pregabalin
(Lyrica™)

What is it?
Pregabalin is an anti-epileptic drug FDA approved for the treatment of seizures and post-herpetic and diabetic nerve pain.

The good news
- Appears to work as well as gabapentin for hot flash relief, but not as well as studied.
- Much better tolerated than gabapentin.

Cautions, side effects, and downsides
- More expensive than gabapentin.
- May impair memory or concentration.

Oxybutynin
Oxytrol™, Ditropan™

What is it?
Oxybutynin is an anticholinergic agent FDA approved for the treatment of overactive bladder.

The good news
- Works very well and reduced hot flashes by up to 75% in two clinical trials as compared with only a 26% reduction in the placebo group.
- Improves both the frequency and severity of flashes.
- Available as a generic.

Cautions, side effects, and downsides
- Dry mouth in up to 50% of women.
- Dementia alert! Anticholinergic drugs block the action of the neurotransmitter acetylcholine and can affect learning and memory. In a 2019 study of 300,000 adults in the U.K., odds of dementia increased nearly 50% among adults age 55 and older who took anticholinergic medication daily for at least three years.

Clonidine
Catapres™, Kapvay™

What is it?
Clonidine is an alpha-2 adrenergic agonist FDA approved for the treatment of hypertension. It is also a sedative.

The good news (not much good news here)
- Available as a generic.

- It's a sedative, so it will help you sleep—hopefully not at your desk when you are trying to get some work done.

Cautions, side effects, and downsides

- I am including clonidine to be complete, but I never prescribe it. The side effects are a real problem, and it doesn't work as well as the other options listed. In fact, clonidine is less effective than all the other drugs listed in this chapter.
- Its ability to lower the number of hot flashes is minimal (38% versus 24% with placebo).
- Side effects include low blood pressure, high blood pressure after stopping it, low heart rate, headache, constipation, dry mouth, dizziness, and sedation.
- The transdermal version may have fewer side effects, but it is also more expensive.

Fezolinetant
(Not available yet!)

What is it?
Fezolinetant is a new class of drugs known as a neurokinin 3 receptor antagonist. The thermoregulatory center in the hypothalamus is controlled by neurokinin 3 receptor neurons, commonly known as KNDy neurons. KNDy neurons are normally regulated by estrogen. After menopause, estrogen declines, and the KNDY neurons go into overdrive. This disruption in the KNDy neuron activation causes hot flashes. Fezolinetant inhibits this overactivity in the KNDy neurons and stops hot flashes from happening.

The good news
- In clinical trials, fezolinetant stops up to 93% of hot flashes!
- Final clinical trials are ongoing, and hopefully fezolinetant will be available in 2023.

Cautions, side effects, and downsides
- *Hopefully* fezolinetant will be available in 2023.
- Side effects are surprisingly minimal. A very small number of women in clinical trials experienced headache, nausea, urinary tract infection, diarrhea, upper respiratory tract infection, and fatigue.

Stellate Ganglion Block

What is it?
The stellate ganglion is a bundle of nerves in the cervical (neck) spinal column. It appears that if a long-acting local anesthetic is injected into this ganglion, hot flashes are reduced for months. As with the other nonhormonal options, it was a serendipitous discovery when women who received a stellate ganglion block for treatment of other conditions noted a dramatic decrease in menopausal hot flashes.

The good news
- Up to a 90% decrease in moderate to very severe hot flashes.
- No medication needs to be taken on a regular basis.

Cautions, side effects, and downsides
- It sounds terrifying, but in truth, it is not a difficult or dangerous procedure in experienced hands. The

stellate ganglion block has been used for over 50 years as a safe and effective treatment for pain and other medical conditions.

- The biggest downside: The procedure needs to be repeated because the effects are temporary, lasting approximately only six months.
- Immediately after the procedure, there is a temporary drooping of the right eyelid, redness in the eye, and congestion in the nose. These are expected effects of the numbing medicine and dissipate within eight hours.
- Most women report that it takes one to two weeks to notice a change in their hot flashes.
- The procedure is not painful and takes only a few minutes, but some women opt to receive conscious sedation (usually with an anti-anxiety medication). If you choose to receive sedation, you will need someone to drive you home after your injection.
- Though available as part of many research studies, stellate ganglion block for the treatment of hot flashes is still considered to be experimental and is not often offered or covered by insurance.

FRANCEY TAKES ADVANTAGE of one of her limited "personal days" (what can be more personal than menopause?) to see Dr. Herpes, who tells her that she is an excellent candidate for hormone therapy. But Francey is particularly worried about the dementia warning and insistent that she wants to try something else first.

After Dr. Herpes explains all the non-estrogen options, Francey decides to go the low-dose Paroxitene route. Though there is no current man in her life, she is relieved to hear that it won't kill what's left of her waning libido.

Eight weeks into her pills, she is still flashing but not soaking the sheets like she was before. It's definitely an improvement, but she is still not getting more than five or six hours of sleep and generally feels less than energetic.

Maybe its time to rethink estrogen therapy- after all it did wonders for her mom, not to mention her own vagina

11

ESTROGEN THERAPY: OF HISTORICAL INTEREST ONLY

I have always been fascinated by medical history. If you have no interest in this stuff, feel free to skip this chapter because it is completely unnecessary. But it is my favorite chapter in the whole book. And if you like it, check out my history section on DrStreicher.com for loads of fun trivia on the history of gynecology, masturbation, tampons, and hysterectomy.

The history of estrogen therapy goes back over 100 years. If there is a theme, it is that the pendulum keeps swinging as we continue to learn why it is important to replace estrogen to ensure quality of life and longevity as well as how best to do it.

Many think that Premarin™ is the beginning of the story, but commercial ventures to replace estrogen and eliminate hot flashes began long before then.

1896
It didn't start with horses; it started with cows. German physicians first prescribed an oral therapy of 5 grams to 20 grams per day of bovine ovarian tissue to women whose ovaries had been surgically removed. They came up with this idea following the success of treating thyroid disorders with extracts from healthy pig and cow thyroid glands.

1907
Merck, an American pharmaceutical company, followed the lead of the German physicians and also pulverized cow ovaries to produce Ovariin Merck. This flavored powder, also available in pill form, was recommended for *"disorders accompanying menopause,"* including *"affections due to atrophy and lesions of the genitals."* Ovariin Merck also promised to relieve *"the very troublesome giddiness, flushing, palpitation, nightmare, loss of memory, insomnia, etc."*

Of note, in the early 1900s, the concept of a clinical trial did not exist. There was no FDA. New drugs were simply released to the public based on the idea that they might work. It also was not unusual for physicians to try a new drug on themselves first, and there is documentation of male doctors taking estrogen just to make sure nothing bad happened. (Evidently, they did not list breast development under the heading of nothing bad.)

1925
Almost 20 years later, the first estrogen product from Organon was released. Ovarnon ointment, manufactured in Amsterdam, was intended to treat menstrual disorders,

but starting in 1927, it was also recommended for the treatment of "menopausal complaints."

1930s

In the early 1930s, almost all commercially distributed estrogen was obtained from the urine (and sometimes placentas) of pregnant women (not horses). Organon, the pharmaceutical company that eventually became Roche-Organon, was the manufacturer of Menformon injections, a truly "bioidentical" hormone therapy extracted from human placental tissue, fetal fluid, and fat from both men and women.

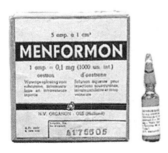

Although brilliant in concept, the reality is that the need for it to be injected, along with the resultant nausea and vomiting, made it intolerable. Menformon was also available in pill form (for maintenance therapy and as a vaginal suppository (Kolpon inserts) intended not only to help with "senior pruritis vulvae" (aka old person's itchy vulva) but also to maintain a healthy, low vaginal pH. Clearly, Organon was well ahead of its time. Kolpon vaginal inserts were also used in children to treat vaginitis.

Menformon dosules, the first transdermal estrogen, was an ointment to be applied "on the skin of the affected area." I was unable to determine if the "affected area" was the genitals, but I assume that to be the case.

At some point, Organon began extracting estrogen from horse urine. Given that it took 25,000 gallons of urine to obtain 1 kilogram (2.2 pounds) of estrogen, it's obvious why the company switched from humans to horses. These products were manufactured in Amsterdam and distributed in the U.S.

During this time period, Progynon™ tablets, produced in Germany, were also initially made from human placenta or ovarian extracts, but the manufacturers eventually switched to urine from pregnant women. Production of this product was, as with Menformon, logistically impractical and expensive because one had to have a lot of women who were willing to donate their ovaries, placentas, or urine.

Progynon 2, the second iteration, was made from the urine of pregnant horses, which was obviously much cheaper and easier than using urine from pregnant women.

In 1934, Ayerst produced Emmenin, which was basically the same thing as Progynon 2, but made in the United States.

The FDA Era Begins

The pharmaceutical world drastically changed when the Food, Drug, and Cosmetic Act was passed by Congress on June 25, 1938. It required that drugs be tested *before* they were brought to market in order to establish safety. The act also mandated that all drugs be labeled with adequate directions for their safe use. This was the beginning of requiring a prescription for drugs. At this point, FDA approval did not require that a drug be proved effective, only that it would not cause harm. It was not until 1962 that a drug had to prove that it worked to gain FDA approval.

1940s

In 1942, Ayerst launched Premarin™ (**Pre**gnant **Mar**es **Urin**e) as a version of Emmenin and Progynon 2. Premarin™ was the first supplemental estrogen to be FDA approved for relief of menopausal symptoms. It was advertised as *"completely natural."* (Sound familiar?)

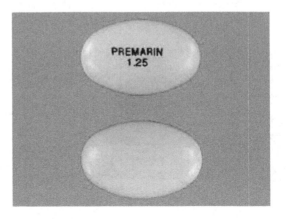

The first consumer article about Premarin™ appeared in a 1948 *Reader's Digest* article titled "New Help for Women's Change of Life."

It is third from the top, right between articles titled, "Why I Remain a Negro" and "Want the Wig?"

The article proclaimed,

"The melancholy sickness that blights the happiness of some women at their change of life [can be] controlled by female hormones; yet most women have gone on suffering. ... But now at last they are ready to transfigure the stormy afternoon of life ... into a time of serenity and vigor."

This was the beginning of an upswing in sales.

1960s

Direct-to-consumer marketing did not exist until 1985, so medical advertisements were directed at physicians and appeared only in medical journals. In the 1960s, Wyeth launched a campaign showing that glamorous, happy women took Premarin™, which in turn resulted in happy husbands. It is no surprise that ads would be directed toward the guys, seeing as back in the 1960s, pretty much every gynecologist was a man. Here is a typical ad to convince gynecologists to prescribe estrogen for their patients:

Husbands, too, like "Premarin."

"Husbands, too, like 'Premarin'"

"The physician who puts a woman on 'Premarin' when she is suffering in the menopause usually makes her pleasant to live with once again. It is no easy thing for a man to take the stings and barbs of business life, then to come home to the turmoil of a woman 'going through the change of life.' If she is not on 'Premarin,' that is. But have her begin estrogen replacement therapy with 'Premarin' ... and [s]he is a happy woman again—something for which husbands are grateful."

Not surprisingly, my physician father put my mother on Premarin™.

But things didn't really take off until Dr. Robert Wilson, the Suzanne Somers of the 1960s, wrote *Feminine Forever*, promising a fountain of sexual, mental, and physical youth to women who treated the "disease" of menopause with estrogen therapy.

Proclaiming that menopause was a disease that required estrogen as treatment, this bestseller stated on its cover that *"every woman, regardless of age, can safely live a full sex life, for her entire life."* I know you will be shocked to hear that this book was funded by Wyeth, the company that made Premarin™, a brilliant direct-to-consumer marketing campaign.

By the late 1960s, the estrogen boom was in full swing, and prescriptions soared.

1970s

By 1970, there were 28 million Premarin™ users. By 1975, it was the fifth-most-prescribed drug in the United States. A first bump in the estrogen road appeared in 1976, when it was realized that women who took estrogen were at increased risk of developing uterine cancer. For the first time, sales dropped.

1980s

In 1980, it was determined that the addition of a progesterone pill to protect the lining of the uterus solved the uterine cancer problem. It is a result of this research why a progestogen (a natural or synthetic form of progesterone) is now routinely prescribed along with estrogen for anyone who has not had a hysterectomy. Conveniently, Provera™, a synthetic progesterone, was already available as contraception and was readily available to prescribe to menopausal women to take with Premarin™. Sales again increased.

Despite the claims of *Feminine Forever*, estrogen was originally intended for—and, in fact, has only ever been FDA-approved specifically for—the treatment of hot flashes and vaginal dryness. But in the 1980s, studies suggested that in addition to helping with bothersome symptoms, post-menopause hormone therapy was also beneficial in preventing heart problems, osteoporosis, and Alzheimer's disease.

In 1984, a National Institutes of Health Consensus Development Conference on Osteoporosis declared estrogens the best way to prevent bone loss.

In the mid-1980s, for the first time, experts were considering prescribing estrogen for benefits beyond symptom relief. The data regarding heart health was front and center because it had long been appreciated that women prior to menopause had a significantly lower risk of developing cardiovascular disease. After menopause, rates were equivalent to those of men. Clearly, estrogen was protective in some way. This concept was supported by the Nurses' Health Study, which concluded that estrogen users have a lower risk of heart disease. But the message was confused by the equally important findings of the Framingham Heart Study, which showed estrogen users have a higher risk of heart disease.

1990

More than 20 small studies supported the finding that heart disease is reduced in menopausal women who use estrogen, and the American College of Physicians recommended that hormone therapy be used by all menopausal women to reduce the risk. So, despite some conflicting data, in the 1990s, we thought we had figured it out. Not only would estrogen eliminate hot flashes, but it also would prolong life. As a result, women were advised to routinely take estrogen during menopause, even if they were asymptomatic.

Sales continued to rise.

2000

By 2000, 20% of post-menopause women were taking hormone therapy. That translates to 90 million prescriptions a year and a $2 *billion* a year industry. In 2001, the FDA approved a combination of Premarin™ and Provera™ in one convenient pill, Prempro™.

July 2, 2002

The day the Women's Health Initiative results were released. The estrogen saga continues in Chapter 14.

BACK TO HER CARDIOLOGIST for a checkup, only to find that though her blood pressure is no longer alarming, her cholesterol is. Her LDL-cholesterol (the bad one), which was teetering on the high side of normal, has now moved into the too-high range. Once again, her cardiologist mentions hormone therapy as not only a way to finally get her flashes under control, but also for heart health. Fortunately, because Francey was just in to see Dr. Herpes, she is able to make a telehealth appointment to discuss hormone therapy options.

The only open telehealth slot is at 3 in the afternoon, so at 2:55, Francey clutches her stomach, mumbles something about "bad sushi," and heads to the bathroom, where she parks herself in a stall and strategically positions her phone so her doctor will not know she is sitting on a toilet during the consultation.

12

ESTROGEN OPTIONS

AS OF NOW, ESTROGEN, even in very small doses, is the most effective treatment of hot flashes and sweats. Period. Estrogen not only works for hot flashes, but it also works fast. Women who start oral or transdermal systemic estrogen replacement generally experience relief within the first few weeks of treatment.

The number one reason most women start systemic estrogen is to treat hot flashes once they realize that practicing yoga, carrying a portable fan, and dressing in layers are not real solutions. Toughing it out works for some women (like the ones who live in Alaska), but others who have severe hot flashes throughout the day and night are blindsided by just how debilitating they can be.

When Is It Time to Start Menopause Hormone Therapy?
Ideally, hormone therapy should be initiated within 10 years of the menopause transition or before age 60. The Women's Health Initiative study (covered in chapter 14) taught us that most of the risks of taking hormone therapy occur in women who start outside of this so-called critical

window. That doesn't mean someone can't start after that time. It just means there needs to be careful consideration of the additional potential risk factors because women starting oral hormone therapy after age 60 have a higher risk of heart disease, stroke, blood clots, and dementia.

Sometimes women are told that they cannot start hormone therapy until they have been without a period for 12 months. That is simply not true. Just because you have not left perimenopause doesn't mean that it is too soon to start HT. The treatment must be individualized and, among other things, is dependent upon whether you are still getting periods.

Once a woman decides that she is going to start post-menopause hormone therapy to extinguish her personal furnace; protect her bones, heart, and brain; and salvage her sleep and sex life, it's decision time!

Before I dive in, I am going to provide some definitions so that we are all speaking the same language.

Systemic estrogens: Intended to work throughout the body to alleviate symptoms such as hot flashes. The blood level you achieve with estrogen therapy is not intended to be as high as when you were 20 (which is why it is called estrogen therapy, or hormone therapy, as opposed to estrogen replacement therapy or hormone replacement therapy) but high enough to alleviate symptoms. A systemic estrogen may be oral (a pill), or it may enter through the skin (transdermal) in the form of a spray, patch, gel, or cream. One vaginal product, Femring™, delivers systemic-level doses in the same range as transdermal and oral products.

Commercially produced bioidentical estrogen: Plant-derived beta-estradiol, which is essentially identical to the estrogen produced by the ovaries. These products are FDA approved and are taken by mouth as a pill; transdermally as a patch, gel, or spray; or via a disposable vaginal ring.

Compounded bioidentical estrogen: Plant-derived beta-estradiol, which is essentially identical to estrogen produced by the ovaries and identical to the estradiol in commercial products. Compounded products are not FDA approved and are distributed by independent compounding pharmacies. Prescribers often recommend multi-hormone regimens and claim that doses are customized and adjusted based on serial hormone-level monitoring. Compounded estrogen is administered through the skin as a lotion or gel or via a pellet placed under the skin. Compounded hormone therapy is covered in detail in chapter 14.

Commercially produced conjugated or synthetic estrogen: Conjugated estrogens are mixtures of manmade or natural estrogens. Synthetic or conjugated estrogens are derived from a plant source. Conjugated equine estrogen is composed of multiple estrogens derived from the urine of pregnant horses. Most of these products are now off the market because of the emergence of bioidentical products.

Local vaginal estrogens: Products placed in the vagina specifically to alleviate the symptoms of vaginal atrophy and genitourinary syndrome of menopause. Though some vaginal estrogen is absorbed into the bloodstream, the amount is minimal, and its effects are local rather than systemic. For that reason, vaginal estrogen has no impact on your hot flashes, bones, or brain. Local vaginal estrogen in the form of a cream, tablet, vaginal ring, insert, or suppository for the treatment of vaginal dryness and painful intercourse is covered in *Slip Sliding Away: Turning Back the Clock On Your Vagina-A gynecologist's guide to eliminating post-menopause dryness and pain.*

All estrogen products are made in a laboratory but if they originate from a plant or animal source are considered to be "natural."

Bioidentical commercial and compounded hormones are both synthesized.

The only thing that is not synthesized is to eat the plant or drink the horse's urine.

This chapter covers all the FDA-approved systemic estrogens. Chapter 13 will cover estrogens that are combined with a progestogen.

All systemic estrogens, whether oral or transdermal, natural, or synthetic, provide:

- Hot flash relief
- A good night's sleep
- Reduction in the risk of osteoporosis and fracture
- Enhanced sexual function (lubrication and genital blood flow, which leads to better libido and ability to orgasm)
- Decreased risk of colon cancer
- Decreased risk of breast cancer
- Less joint pain and stiffness
- Decreased brain fog
- Decrease in risk of type 2 diabetes
- Decrease in visceral (organ) fat
- A favorable effect on body fat distribution and increase in lean body mass
- Fewer wrinkles (Not life-threatening, but I thought you would like to know)

None of the estrogen-alone options increases the risk of breast cancer but, on the contrary, decreases it. Many risks and benefits are dependent on whether you are taking *estrogen alone* or *combined with a progesterone*. The timing of *when* you initiate hormone therapy is also important. Chapter 14 will get into the details along with the risks of hormone therapy and compounded products and pellets.

Transdermal vs. Oral vs. Vaginal: There Is a Difference
When most women think about hormone therapy, they assume they will be receiving a pill, but that is no longer the case. In the 1980s, transdermal patches were developed as an alternative means of delivering estrogen. Now, in addition to estrogen patches, there are also sprays, gels, and lotions that are applied to the arm or thigh daily. In 2003, Femring™ (not to be confused with Estring™), a slow-release vaginal ring, hit the market as the next FDA-approved, safe, and effective way to deliver systemic estrogen. Oral, vaginal, and transdermal estrogen all alleviate hot flashes and support bone health, but there are major differences that go beyond symptom relief. Convenience, your medical history, your personal preference, and your insurance coverage are all considerations, but what's most important when choosing an estrogen is safety and efficacy.

Oral
Although some oral options are synthetic or derived from horse urine, all the newer products are derived from plants and are bioidentical to the estrogen produced by ovaries. All oral estrogens are effective. The major advantage of an oral option is convenience: It's easy to swallow a pill. The disadvantage, when compared to the non-oral products, is that oral options are metabolized by the liver. That

trip through the liver is what results in risk factors that are unique to oral estrogen.

Benefits that are *specific* to **oral** estrogen products include:

- Convenience of swallowing a pill.
- Decrease cholesterol (even more than transdermal products).
- Increase in HDL-C ("good") cholesterol as well as decrease in LDL-C ("bad") cholesterol.

Risks *specific* to **oral** estrogen products include:

- Increase in gall stones.
- Increase in coagulation factors, upping the risk of blood clots.
- Increase in inflammatory markers associated with heart disease.
- Increase in triglyceride levels.
- Increase in risk of blood clots.
  - Stroke (ischemic, not hemorrhagic).
  - Pulmonary embolism.
  - Deep vein thrombosis.
- Increase in sex hormone binding globulin (SHBG), which decreases the amount of active testosterone.

This sounds concerning—OK, terrifying—but it is important to put it in perspective. Most low-risk women do just fine taking pills. It is also worth noting that most women avoid estrogen because of a fear of breast cancer. What they should be worried about is the risk of a blood clot. But even those numbers are small. If you consider the number of potential side effects from taking birth control pills, most women would never take them, but only a very small number have problems.

Transdermal

The primary advantage of transdermal estrogen is that when the skin absorbs it, it goes directly into the bloodstream and bypasses the gastrointestinal system. Originally transdermal products were developed to benefit women who had liver or gallbladder disease known to be aggravated by oral estrogen. It soon became clear that avoiding the trip through the liver included other benefits, primarily the elimination of the increased risk of blood clots and stroke associated with oral estrogen.

Blood clots are more likely to occur in the deep veins of the legs of women who have high cholesterol and triglycerides. All estrogens decrease cholesterol, but oral estrogens increase triglycerides, and transdermal estrogens decrease triglycerides.

Also increasing the chance that blood will form into dangerous clots is the presence of high levels of clotting factors such as fibrinogen and factor 7. Transdermal estrogens decrease fibrinogen and factor 7. In addition, a protein produced in the liver called C-reactive protein causes blood clots to grow larger and more prone to breaking away and traveling to distant blood vessels. Oral estrogens increase C-reactive protein. Transdermal estrogens do not.

Another underappreciated advantage is that transdermal estrogen absorbed through the skin as a patch, spray, or gel, has a more favorable impact on libido than oral estrogen. Here's why: Estrogen pills increase sex hormone-binding globulin (SHBG), a protein that binds testosterone (essential for libido!) and makes it inactive. So a high SHBG reduces the amount of active testosterone and reduces your desire for sex. Women who lose their libido while taking birth control pills are familiar with this phenomenon. If you are taking oral estrogen therapy and have a lagging libido, you may want to talk to your doctor about switching to a transdermal option.

All transdermal products are plant-derived and bioidentical.

Benefits *specific* to **transdermal** estrogen products include:
- No effect on liver or gallbladder.
- Decrease in inflammatory markers (fibrinogen, C-reactive protein, factor 7).
- No increase in SHBG.
- Lowers insulin resistance.
- No increase in triglycerides.
- No increase in the risk of blood clots, stroke, pulmonary embolism, or deep vein thrombosis.
- Neutral or beneficial effect on cholesterol, LDL-C, and HDL-C.
- Estrogen levels are consistent and stable.

Risks *specific* to **transdermal** estrogen products include:
- Skin irritation.
- Possibility of skin-to-skin transfer with contact less than one hour after application of estrogen gel or lotion.

Transvaginal

When women think of vaginal estrogen, there are generally referring to the administration of local vaginal estrogen for the treatment of vaginal dryness. But the vagina is also an excellent way of delivering *systemic* estrogen—in dosages that have the same benefits of taking an oral or transdermal product. Currently, FemRing™ is the only vaginal estrogen product for systemic therapy to decrease hot flashes. Just to be clear, the other vaginal ring, Estring™, one of the local vaginal estrogens, is only for the treatment of vaginal dryness and painful intercourse due to genitourinary syndrome of menopause (the topic of *Slip Sliding Away*) and will not help your flashes, your bones, or your brain. Femring™ is NOT the same as Estring™! The risks and benefits that are specific to the transdermal products also hold for Femring™, because as with the transdermal products, it is not metabolized by the liver.

Although the vaginal ring has never caught on to the same extent as the transdermal products, I think that will change as more women, and doctors, become aware of it. Even more important, as a generation of women who used NuvaRing™ for contraception enter menopause, the concept of taking hormones via the vagina will be more familiar and more acceptable.

Comparison of Transdermal and Oral Estrogen

	Oral estrogen	Transdermal estrogen
Triglycerides	↑	← or ↓
Total cholesterol	↓↓	↓
HDL-C	↑↑	↑
LDL-C	↓↓	↓
Risk of blood clots (stroke, pulmonary embolism, deep vein thrombosis)	↑	←
Sex hormone binding globulin	↑	←
Insulin resistance	↓	↓
Cardiac inflammatory factors	↑	↓
Affects liver/gallbladder	↑	←

← No different than in women who do not take estrogen.

↑ Increased when compared to women who do not take estrogen.

↓ Decreased when compared to women who do not take estrogen.

A Word About Class Labeling

If you are someone who reads the fine print before you take a new medicine, the list of risks on your estrogen product will convince you that it is not worth getting blood clots, cancer, and dementia to get rid of your hot flashes. But FDA class labeling requires all products with the same ingredient to have the same warning, even if the risk has never been demonstrated in a particular product. In other words, just because something is listed as a risk doesn't mean it is a risk. For example, taking oral systemic estrogens can increase the risk of developing a blood clot. That risk has never been demonstrated in the use of a transdermal estrogen product; nevertheless, the FDA requires that a blood clot warning be on every product that contains estrogen. Virtually every one of the warnings on transdermal or vaginal estrogen labels is based on the risks associated with systemic oral estrogen. Read chapter 14. You will feel much better.

The Products

Though it is tempting to go through the list and pick the most appealing product, several variables should impact your decision, including medical risk factors, which progestogen you take (see chapter 13), your insurance benefits, and, of course, your personal preference. What this list will do is give you an idea of the types of products available, along with some pros and cons of each. That way, when you have a discussion with your doctor about your best option, you will be armed with information.

Oral Products

Conjugated Equine Estrogen
Premarin™

What it is: Conjugated equine estrogen is prepared from the urine of pregnant mares and is composed of at least 10 different estrogens with unique estrogen-receptor affinities and potencies, among which estradiol represents less than 1%.

The good side:
- There is no evidence that estrogen derived from horse urine is any less safe or effective than estrogen derived from plants.
- Conjugated equine estrogen is a natural source of estrogen. I know, the perception is that it is not as natural as estrogen from a plant. But what could be more natural than horse pee? Not to mention, humans are a lot closer to horses than we are to plants.
- There are none of the concerns associated with transdermal estrogen, such as skin reactions or the possibility of transferring estrogen to another person. There are no precautions about washing, sunscreen, or moisturizer application.

The bad side:
- It's not bioidentical (which has never proven to be a problem, but I am including it as a "bad side" because many women prefer to use a plant-derived bioidentical product).
- It has the risks associated with oral estrogen that were listed earlier.

- One cannot measure estrogen levels while taking it because the product contains multiple types of estrogens.
- The horse problem. Per the People for the Ethical Treatment of Animals (PETA) website, *"Tied in small stalls, unable to move either backward, forwards, or sideways or lie down comfortably, they stand with sacks strapped to their groins for months on end. To make the urine more concentrated, their water intake is restricted, so the horses are constantly thirsty. The foals are considered "byproducts," and most are fattened up, slaughtered, and sold for horsemeat or turned into dog food."* There is no proof of any of this, and the manufacturer, Wyeth Ayerst, insists that the horses are treated humanely. The farms that breed these horses adhere to a strict code of ethics that addresses the issues of exercise, water intake, nutrition, housing, and veterinary care of the broodmares.

Nonetheless, many animal lovers feel very strongly about avoiding Premarin for this reason alone.

Oral Synthetic Estrogen
Estropipate (generic), Cenestin™ Menest™

What they are: Estropipate is synthesized from plant material. It is metabolized in the body into estradiol and estrone. It originally was marketed as Ogen™ and Ortho-EST™ but is now only available as a generic. Cenestin™ is conjugated synthetic estrogen. Menest™, an esterified estrogen, is a mixture of sodium salts of the sulfate esters of estrogenic substances.

The good side:
- There is no evidence that estropipate synthesized from plants is any less safe or effective than bioidentical

estrogen, particularly because it is metabolized into a bioidentical hormone.

- Ditto: There is no evidence that conjugated synthetic estrogens or esterified estrogen is any less safe or effective than bioidentical estrogen.
- There are none of the concerns associated with transdermal products, such as skin reactions or the possibility of transferring estrogen to another person. There are no precautions about washing, sunscreen, or moisturizer application.

The bad side:
- They are not bioidentical (which has never proven to be a problem, but I am including it as a "bad side" because many women prefer to use a plant-derived bioidentical product).
- They have all the risks associated with oral estrogen that were listed earlier.
- They are not commonly used and often not available.

Oral Estradiol
Estrace™

What it is: Oral estradiol is plant-derived bioidentical estradiol.

The good side:
- It's bioidentical.
- There are none of the concerns associated with transdermal products, such as skin reactions and the possibility of transferring estrogen to another person. There are no precautions about washing, sunscreen, or moisturizer application.

- It's available as a generic.

The bad side:
- It has all the risks associated with oral estrogen, which were listed earlier.

Transdermal Products

The following list includes all non-oral estrogen products intended for systemic therapy that are FDA approved to alleviate hot flashes and prevent bone loss. If you have a uterus, you must also take a progestogen to prevent an abnormal buildup of tissue. Transdermal combination products with both a progestogen and estrogen are covered in chapter 13.

Patches
Alora™, Climera™, Esclim™, Estraderm™, Menostar™, Minivelle™, Vivelle™, Vivelle-dot™, generics

What they are: Each product is a round or square patch, in varying sizes, that adheres to the skin and slowly releases estradiol. Depending on the brand, the patch is changed either once or twice a week. The patch should be applied to the lower abdomen or upper buttock in a hair-free area sans powder, oil, or lotion. When it is time to replace the patch, a new one should be applied to a different area of skin.

There are three technologies used to manufacture patches:

Reservoir: The estrogen is in a small reservoir in the patch that has an alcohol membrane that controls the rate of release.

Matrix: There is a suspension of estrogen that is in direct contact with the skin. The adhesive is only on the perimeter.

Dot-matrix: This combines the adhesive and estrogen in one layer. These patches are the smallest, thinnest, and, of course, most expensive.

The good side:

- Unlike pills, which must be taken daily, patches offer the advantage of needing to be used only once or twice a week.
- Generics are available and are often less expensive than other transdermal products.
- Unlike with other transdermal products, there are no concerns about transferring estrogen to others you come in contact with.

The bad side:

- Some women don't like to wear a patch.
- Patches can irritate the skin. This is especially true with a reservoir patch.
- Patches generally do not come off in the shower or the pool, but sometimes they do.
- Sometimes a patch comes off even if it does not get wet.
- Patches should not be exposed to direct sunlight because high temperatures can affect the release rate of estrogen.
- Patches can look dirty and can leave behind sticky residue.
- Patches do come as generics, but they are usually larger and more irritating than the trade-name products.

Gels/Creams
Divigel™, Elestrin™, EstroGel™, Estrasorb™

What they are: Estradiol gels and lotions were designed to avoid the skin irritation problem common with patches. They are applied daily.

Elestrin™ and **EstroGel™** are clear gels packaged in a canister that deliver a specific amount per pump. These gels are pumped into your hand and then applied to the arm, from wrist to shoulder.

Divigel™ gel is packaged in individual foil packets and applied to the thigh.

Estrasorb™ is a lotion in a soy-based oil preparation packaged in individual foil packets. It is applied to the legs, thighs, or calves.

The good side:
- Creams and gels avoid the sticky residue and skin reactions experienced by some women with the patch.
- It is easy to titrate the dosage up or down without getting a new prescription.
- The varieties that come in packets are great for travel or to throw in a bag because they take up very little space.

The bad side:
- The gels are alcohol-based, and there is a chance that you will burst into flame if you light a cigarette (one more reason not to smoke).
- Creams and gels are often more expensive than patches.
- The gels can be transferred to someone else if there is direct contact before they have dried (two to five minutes) and been completely absorbed (about one hour).

- You must wait *at least* an hour before washing the area. Some studies show decreased absorption if the area is washed one hour later.
- They can get on your clothes if you get dressed before they're completely dry.

Spray
Evamist™

What it is: Evamist™ is estradiol sprayed on the skin between the elbow and the wrist on the inside of the forearm.

The good side:
- The spray dries more quickly than gel varieties, which means you can get dressed within two minutes and wash the area within 30 minutes.
- You do not need to put the product on your fingers to apply or rub it in, which means you don't need to wash your hands, and there is less chance to transfer it to other areas or other people.

The bad side:
- The spray is alcohol-based, and there is a chance that you will burst into flame if you light a cigarette—but only for a few minutes.
- It is generally more expensive than patches.
- It has been associated with adverse effects in children who were exposed to the drug via skin contact. There have been eight cases of unintended exposure in children ages 3 to 5 years old that resulted in nipple swelling and breast development in girls and breast enlargement in boys, which occurred weeks to months after the drug was initiated in the adult. If you are spending time with small children,

consider wearing long sleeves or at least make sure your estrogen has dried before any major hugging or holding.

- There have been reports of adverse effects in pets exposed to the drug via skin contact, such as mammary/nipple enlargement and vulvar swelling. In other words, best to not let your dog lick your arm after you have applied your estrogen.

Vaginal Ring
Femring™

What it is: Femring™ is *systemic* (not local) estrogen and is intended for the treatment of hot flashes. It will also treat vaginal dryness, but this dose is higher than necessary for that purpose. If you are only treating vaginal dryness, Femring™ is not needed. Estring™ is the product that is a lower-dose estrogen only intended to treat vaginal dryness (it's covered in detail in *Slip Sliding Away*). Femring™ is a flexible, silastic, disposable ring that you insert in the vagina and replace every three months. It slowly releases estradiol.

One size fits all. You simply fold the flexible 2-inch ring or twist it into a figure-8 shape and give a little push, so it slips into the back of the vagina. The position is not important if once it is in, you cannot feel it and are not aware of it. It does not need to be removed during intercourse (although you can if you want to), and it is the rare guy who can feel it. When it's time for removal, you use your fingers to pull it out. Every three months you remove it yourself, throw it away, and replace it with another Femring™.

The good side:
- Set it and forget it: You need to replace it only every 3 months.

- Femring™ comes in two doses.
- It has all the benefits of transdermal products without the skin reactions or the possibility of transferring estrogen to another person.
- There are no precautions about washing, sunscreen, or moisturizer application.

The bad side:
- Some women have difficulty putting it in place.
- Some women find it difficult to remove. I do have a handful of patients who come in and have me do it for them. Alternatively, you can tie a length of dental floss ribbon (unminted!) to the ring, tuck the floss into your vagina once you place the ring, and, when it is time for removal, fish out the floss, and use it to pull the ring down so it is easily reachable.

BECAUSE OF FRANCEY'S HIGH BLOOD PRESSURE and heart history, Dr. Herpes recommends that she use a transdermal product. After hearing all the options, she decides to go for the very cool-looking estradiol spray.

Following her bathroom stall telemedicine appointment, Francey unnecessarily flushes the toilet and goes through the optics of washing her hands when she hears another flush. The manager of the museum gift shop emerges from the stall next to hers and tells Francey that if the spray doesn't work out, the little foil packets are her go-to. Francey is shocked—this woman can't be more than 35, and she is taking hormone therapy? The shock must have shown on her face, because the woman goes on to explain that she went through menopause last year after completing chemotherapy for anal cancer. Clearly HT is not just something "old people" take.

On the way home, Francey fills her prescription for the spray and micronized progesterone to take at bedtime. Two weeks later, she's still flashing but better. Per Dr. Herpes' instructions, she bumps up to two sprays a day with guidance that she may need to go to three.

How to **Monitor Treatment**

It is not necessary, or helpful, to routinely measure hormone levels in a woman taking standard doses of hormone therapy. A specific hormone level may provide one woman total relief of her symptoms. Other women might need a higher level to get the same effect. Using saliva to test hormone levels (discussed in chapter 2), not to mention repeating the test at regular intervals to see if hormone replacement is "working" or to adjust dosage, is often just another example of profit-motivated entrepreneurs taking advantage of vulnerable women who are only trying to take hormones in a safe, responsible way.

The best indicator that you are taking enough estrogen is how you feel. The fact that you no longer have hot flashes, vaginal dryness, mood swings, or insomnia and can remember why you walked into a room is a better indication that you are taking the right amount of estrogen than any laboratory test.

Having said that, evaluating blood levels during treatment is sometimes useful.

If you are taking standard levels of hormone replacement drugs yet continue to have symptoms, a blood test is helpful to see if you are in the range expected to relieve flashes. If your levels are low, you can increase the dosage or, in some cases, might find it beneficial to change the delivery mechanism. If your blood levels are well within the range that should alleviate symptoms, it is time to consider if your flashes are because of a medical problem not related to menopause.

Most important, if you are feeling good and are flash-free, there is no reason to routinely check hormone levels. Many doctors who prescribe compounded HT or pellets routinely check levels, but in truth, this is not useful or necessary. More on that in chapter 14.

When Is It Time to Stop?

You may have heard that hormone therapy should be taken at the "lowest dose for the shortest amount of time". Or maybe you were told that after five years, you must stop taking it. Neither of those recommendations is based on science, and, in fact, most menopause experts strongly disagree, particularly in the case of women who enter menopause at a young age because of premature ovarian insufficiency, surgical menopause, or cancer treatments.

A few years ago, I was asked to moderate a panel for the annual meeting of the North American Menopause Society. The idea was to have a discussion among academic menopause experts to determine how long someone should take hormone therapy. I contacted my cadre of experts and asked if they would be interested in participating. One hundred percent agreed to be on the panel. When I asked them which position they wanted to defend, "take hormone therapy until death" or "take hormone therapy for five years," *100%* would participate only if they were on the "take hormone therapy until death" side. I had to change the topic of the panel.

So, the answer to "How long a woman should take HT?" According to the experts? Death is a good time to stop.

The 2017 North American Menopause Society hormone therapy position statement on the topic is as follows:

"The recommendation to routinely discontinue hormone therapy is NOT supported by scientific data. Decisions to continue hormones beyond age 60 should be individualized."

FAQ

Q: How long do I need to wait to wash after I apply estrogen gel, spray, or cream?

A: If possible, apply your estrogen after, not before, you shower. If using a gel, you should wait at least an hour; a spray, 30 minutes.

Q: How long do I need to wait to apply sunscreen after I apply estrogen gel, spray, or cream?

A: Again, better to apply your sunscreen before. One study using Estrogel™ showed a 16% decrease in absorption of estrogen if sunscreen is applied one hour afterward.

Q: How long do I need to wait to apply moisturizing lotion after I apply estrogen gel, spray, or cream?

A: Although sunscreen decreases absorption, moisturizers increase absorption by as much as 73%! Wait at least two hours, or better, apply before.

Q: Can a patch be cut in half?

A: It depends on the technology used to make it. If a reservoir patch (common in generics) is cut, the estrogen will seep out. Most patches use a matrix technology that theoretically can be cut, but, of course, the manufacturer does not recommend it.

Q: What do I do if a patch comes off?

A: You can put it back on but apply it to a different area. If it won't stick, use a new patch.

Q: My insurance doesn't cover the product I want to use. Any ideas?

A: Start by trying to justify to your insurance why you need the preferred product. ("The patch made my skin red and itchy.") Also, product websites often have copay cards and deals. GoodRx.com is a website that compares prices at neighborhood pharmacies and can send coupons to your phone.

Q: I am using estrogen but still flashing. Now what?

A: First, you may need a higher dose. If you continue to have problems, checking your blood hormone level will determine if you are absorbing it and metabolizing it correctly. Also, if you are using a transdermal gel, make sure you are not washing the area too soon or applying sunscreen on top of it. If you continue to flash despite what appears to be adequate hormone levels, you may be experiencing hot flashes or night sweats for another reason. In any case, this is a situation to be discussed with your doctor.

Q: If I choose to stop my hormone therapy, do I need to taper off or can I just stop?

A: You can just stop. Sometimes women are advised to taper to decrease the chance of getting hot flashes. That is ridiculous. If you are going to have a return of hot flashes after stopping estrogen, tapering will not help. It will just take them longer to start back up.

Q: Can I take my hormone therapy every other day instead of every day?

A: A lot of my patients ask about that to save money. You can, but particularly if you are taking oral estrogen, you will be more likely to flash (or bleed) than if you were to take a smaller dose every day.

Q: I want to switch from oral Premarin™ to a transdermal product. How do I know what dose to use?

A: Because transdermal estrogen is available in different strengths and delivery systems (patch, pump, packets), dosing equivalents are tricky. There have been no studies that compare different products directly. Most experienced menopause experts can determine an equivalent dose. Sometimes it helps to measure blood estradiol levels to get to the right adjustment.

Q: What if I miss a dose?

A: Unlike with birth control pills, a missed dose is not potentially catastrophic. The worst that will happen is you might have some spotting, breakthrough bleeding, or hot flashes.

Q: I started HT at age 50 but was told to stop at age 55 by my internist. I am now 61 and still flashing and miserable, but I can't get anyone to prescribe me any because I am over 60. Is it safe for me to restart after being off for six years?

A: This is one of the most common questions we get at the clinic. The answer is, probably. There is limited data on this scenario, so the decision to restart HT is based on individual risk factors.

Q: If I am using two pumps of estrogen gel, or two sprays of Evamist, where do I put the second dose?

In the case of the gel, you should apply one dose to each arm. The second shot of estrogen spray can be applied to the same arm, but not at the same spot.

Q: Any tricks to get off the sticky residue my patch leaves behind?

A: Apply baby oil, then wait a few minutes, and it should wipe off easily.

Q: Can I apply a transdermal estrogen to a different area than the directions say?

A: I get it. You just put on your pantyhose, skirt, and belt only to discover that you forgot to put your Divigel™ on your thigh. Or you want to use Evamist™, but you are worried because you will be carrying around your 1-year-old granddaughter. It is probably OK to put it somewhere else, but realize that in the clinical trials, the absorption and the anticipated blood levels of the hormone were based on consistent application to a designated spot.

Q: I like my patch, but my skin gets red and irritated. Am I allergic to estrogen?

A: You probably are reacting to the adhesive, which is more likely if you are using a generic. If you can switch to a patch with dot-matrix technology, a reaction is much less likely. Otherwise, a gel or spray may be in your future.

Q: I never felt good when I was taking birth control pills. Does that mean I will have problems taking hormone therapy?

A: The amount and potency of hormones in hormone therapy are dramatically lower than in birth control pills, so it is unlikely that you will have the same reaction.

Q: I'm bleeding!

A: Don't panic. In 90% of cases, bleeding while taking hormone therapy is not an indication of anything serious. Having said that, never ignore bleeding. Let your prescriber know so they can do appropriate testing to see if you need to change anything or do anything.

FOUR WEEKS INTO HORMONE THERAPY, Francey is flash-free and sleeping through the night. Her head is clear, work is going great, and she is even thinking about renewing her Match.com subscription. The only thing that is not going well is that she still can't zip her jeans. Convinced it is the progesterone that is responsible, she takes herself off it for a couple of weeks and loses 3 pounds. It's a tough call: preventing uterine cancer versus vanity.

13

PROTECTING YOUR UTERUS

ONE IN FOUR WOMEN in the United States has had a hysterectomy, and if you belong to that club, you can skip this chapter. But if you own a uterus and take systemic estrogen, you also need to take steps to prevent an abnormal buildup in the lining of the uterus. For those of you who skipped chapter 11, this was a lesson learned in the 1980s. Before that, estrogen was given alone, resulting in an increased risk of endometrial (uterine) cancer.

Menstruating women make progesterone.

Post-menopause women need to take progesterone.

Before menopause, the ovaries pump out estrogen, and once ovulation (egg release) occurs, they also produce progesterone to prepare the lining of the uterus in the event that a fertilized egg is going to land there. If pregnancy does not occur, progesterone levels drop at the time of menstruation. If a young woman produces estrogen but does not ovulate, she is at risk of an abnormal buildup in the lining of the uterus—and for uterine cancer.

Likewise, if a post-menopause woman is taking estrogen but not taking progesterone, she has a tenfold risk of developing uterine cancer.

But good news: When a woman takes progesterone with estrogen therapy, she decreases her risk of uterine cancer below that of a woman who does not take hormones at all. The progesterone is protective. But...

The Progesterone **Problem**

Although most women do fine when they take a synthetic or natural progesterone, many women experience less-than-pleasant side effects, such as moodiness and bloating. In addition, it matters which product you use because some, in addition to potentially making you feel awful, are also associated with an increased risk of medical problems.

Before I move forward with the nitty-gritty of the specific products, here is a glossary to clarify confusing terminology.

Progesterone: The *naturally occurring hormone* normally produced by the ovaries after a woman ovulates.

Progestin: Any *synthetic* form of progesterone. Progestins are commonly used in hormonal contraception, such as birth control pills, implants, and IUDs, but they are also used in lower doses for menopause hormone therapy.

Progestins used in FDA-approved products include drospirenone, levonorgestrel, medroxyprogesterone acetate (MPA), norethindrone acetate, and norgestinate.

Progestogen: A general term that includes all compounds that bind to progesterone receptors. Progestogens include *both* naturally occurring progesterone and synthetic progestins.

FDA-Approved Products

There are two FDA-approved, standalone oral progesto-gens for endometrial protection: *medroxyprogesterone acetate* and *micronized progesterone*. The appropriate dose is dependent on the estrogen dose.

Medroxyprogesterone Acetate (MPA)
Provera™

What it is:
- An oral progestin.
- Historically, the most prescribed synthetic progestin.
- Used in most studies, including the Women's Health Initiative Study (or WHI; see chapter 14).

The good side:
- Effectively prevents abnormal buildup in the lining of the uterus.
- Inexpensive, and available as a generic.
- Can be combined with either a standalone transdermal estrogen or oral estrogen.
- Makes some women sleepy, which can help with insomnia.
- Helps build bone beyond the benefit seen with estrogen so may be preferable in women at risk for osteoporosis
- Multiple dosing options (1.25 mg, 2.5 mg, 5 mg, and 10 mg).

The bad side:
- Although most women feel fine, many experience bloating, water retention, fatigue, and moodiness.
- Makes some women sleepy.
- Some women gain weight secondary to water retention.

- Long-term use is associated with an increased risk of breast cancer (see chapter 14).
- Diminishes beneficial cardiac effects of estrogen, and is associated with an increased risk of coronary heart disease.
- Eliminates the benefit of estrogen on blood flow.
- Negative effect on lipids.

Micronized Progesterone (MP)
Prometrium™

What it is:
- A "bioidentical" progesterone, meaning that it is chemically identical to the progesterone made by human ovaries.
- Thought of as natural because it utilizes precursors of progesterone found in wild yams in the production process. But strictly speaking, it is chemically synthesized using natural products.

The good side:
- Effectively prevents abnormal buildup in the lining of the uterus.
- Very inexpensive, and available as a generic.
- Can be combined with either a standalone transdermal or oral estrogen.
- Most women tolerate micronized progesterone much better than MPA.
- Not associated with an increase in lipids or risk of cardiovascular disease.
- Not associated with an increased risk of breast cancer.
- Does not cause weight gain.
- Preferred by most menopause experts over MPA.

The bad side:
- Most women tolerate micronized prometrium much better than MPA, but some women still experience bloating, water retention, fatigue, and moodiness.
- Limited dosing options (100 mg and 200 mg).

Norethindrone Acetate (NETA)

What it is:
Norethindrone Acetate is an oral synthetic progestin that is often used alone in higher doses to treat endometriosis, abnormal bleeding and for contraception. In lower doses it is used alone or in combination with estrogen for endometrial protection and sometimes to treat vasomotor symptoms.

The good side:
- Effectively prevents abnormal buildup in the lining of the uterus.
- Helps build bone beyond the benefit seen with estrogen so may be preferable in women at risk for osteoporosis
- Inexpensive, and available as a generic.

Can be combined with either a standalone transdermal estrogen or oral estrogen.

The bad side:
- Limited dosing options (0.5 mg, 1 mg).
- Most women tolerate NETA much better than MPA, but some women still experience bloating, water retention, fatigue, and moodiness.

Combination Products

Combination products contain both estrogen and progestogen. This is the same concept as birth control pills but in much lower doses. In other words, though the ingredients may look the same as those of a birth control pill, these products will NOT provide contraception because the dose is much lower. Combination HT is FDA approved in the form of a patch or a pill.

Oral Estrogen and Progestin Combinations
Conjugated equine estrogens and medroxyprogesterone acetate (**Prempro™**), Estradiol and drospirenone (**Angeliq™**), Estradiol and micronized progesterone (**Bijuva™**), Estradiol and norgestimate (**Prefest™**), Estradiol and norethindrone acetate (**Activella™**, **Amabelz ™**, **Mimvey™**), Ethinyl estradiol and norethindrone acetate (**FemHRT™**, **Jevantique Lo™**)

What they are:
Pills taken daily that contain both estrogen and progestogen.

The good side:
- Convenient.
- Effectively prevent abnormal buildup in the lining of the uterus.
- Many choices are available, some of which may be tolerated better than others.
- A bioidentical combination is available. Bijuva™ contains estradiol and micronized progesterone in one pill, which is more convenient than taking two products separately.

The bad side:
- All the issues discussed with oral estrogens in chapter 12.
- All the issues discussed with progestogens.
- No generic equivalent as a combination pill.

Transdermal Estrogen and Progestin Combinations
Estradiol and norethindrone (**Combipatch™**),
Estradiol and levonorgestrol (**Climera Pro ™**)

What they are:
- Adhesive patches applied to the lower abdomen or buttocks that continuously release estrogen and progestogen.
- Combipatch™ is changed twice weekly.
- Climera Pro™ is changed once weekly.

The good side:
- Some women find placing a patch once or twice a week to be more convenient than taking a daily pill.
- They effectively prevent abnormal buildup in the lining of the uterus.
- Potentially fewer side effects than with oral progestins.
- All the advantages of a transdermal estrogen, as discussed in chapter 12.

The bad side:
- Some women find placing a patch once or twice a week to be less convenient than taking a daily pill because they need to keep track and remember to change it.
- Some patches tend to be on the large side (Frisbee, anyone?)
- More breakthrough bleeding.
- Skin reactions in 2% to 6% of users.

- A patch should not be placed where a clothing waist-band will rub against it because it might come off.
- Many women are concerned that a patch will come off with sweating or exercise. This is not common, but if it does occur, a new patch must be placed (in a different spot!)
- No generic equivalent.

Progestin Alternatives

If you are in the group that does not tolerate progestin, or if you are concerned about a long-term breast cancer risk, there are alternatives short of a hysterectomy!

Bazodoxifene
Duavee™

Bazodoxifene is a selective estrogen receptor modulator, also known as a SERM. SERMs are drugs that either block estrogen pathways or activate estrogen pathways in specific tissues.

There are lots of SERMS you may be familiar with:
- Clomiphene (Clomid™) stimulates ovarian tissue and is used as a fertility drug.
- Tamoxifen blocks estrogen pathways in the breast, which is why it is useful in the prevention of breast cancer.
- Raloxifene (Evista™) stimulates estrogen pathways in bone (to treat osteopenia and osteoporosis) and blocks estrogen pathways in the breast (to prevent breast cancer).
- Ospemifene (Osphena™) stimulates estrogen pathways in vaginal and vulvar tissue and essentially has the

same effect as local vaginal estrogen in alleviating painful intercourse and vaginal dryness due to menopause.

Bazodoxifene is a SERM that blocks estrogen pathways in the uterine lining and, therefore, does a great job of protecting the uterine lining. As a bonus, it also builds bone and prevents osteoporosis. And though it is not FDA approved to protect breast tissue, in laboratory testing it blocks estrogen receptors in the breast.

Bazodoxifene is the *perfect* option for a woman who wants to protect her uterus, protect her bones, and protect her breasts.

Duavee™ is the only FDA-approved option that contains bazodoxifene, and women who choose it get the benefit of estrogen without the risk of taking a progestin. But there's a downside. Of course.

Bazodoxifene cannot be prescribed as a standalone drug. It only comes combined with oral conjugated equine estrogens (Premarin™). That's because the company that patented bazodoxifene is the same company that makes Premarin™. So to get the benefit of bazodoxifene, you must also be willing to take an oral estrogen conjugated from horse urine. For a lot of women, that is less than ideal, both medically and ideologically. Also, it only comes in one dose, and in the world of menopause hormone therapy, one dose does not fit all.

Bazodoxifene and Conjugated Equine Estrogen
Duavee™

What it is:
- Selective estrogen receptor modulator (SERM) combined with conjugated equine estrogens (Premarin™).
- Once-daily pill.

The good side:

- Effectively prevents abnormal buildup in the lining of the uterus.
- Avoids negative aspects of taking a progestogen.
- Builds bone.
- Convenient.
- Protects breast tissue and potentially decreases the risk of breast cancer (still under investigation; see chapter 15).

The bad side:

- Only available combined with oral conjugated equine estrogens (Premarin™).
- Only available in one dose.
- Not always covered by insurance.
- No generic equivalent.

Off-Label Options

The number one off-label option I offer my patients is the placement of a levonorgestrel-releasing intrauterine device (IUD) in the uterus. For a long time, women were reluctant to consider this possibility, but after actress Angelina Jolie went public with her ovary removal and subsequent menopause journey and revealed that to be *her* plan, suddenly it became far more acceptable. Yet another example of the power of celebrity over the power of expertise, but I digress.

For many women who do not tolerate or wish to avoid a progestin, a progestin releasing IUD is the ideal alternative. Many studies demonstrate, and many experts believe, that an IUD provides better uterine protection than achieved using an oral progestogen and should always be the preferred approach. Though it's the standard in Europe, it is not yet FDA approved here and is, therefore, an "off-label" practice.

Levonorgestrel-Releasing Intrauterine Device (LNG-IUD)
Mirena™, Liletta™

What it is:
- A small, T-shaped plastic device embedded with levonorgestrel that a health care professional places in the uterine cavity.
- Levonorgestrel is slowly released into the uterine cavity
- Currently FDA approved only for contraception and to treat heavy bleeding.
- Mirena™ and Liletta™ each have 52 mg of levonorgestrel. Kyleena™ and Skyla™ have lower amounts and are not generally used for endometrial protection.

The good side:
- Provides very high levels of intrauterine progestin.
- Effectively prevents abnormal buildup in the lining of the uterus.
- Very low systemic absorption, and, therefore, side effects seen with oral progestins are rare.
- Can be combined with either a standalone transdermal estrogen or oral estrogen.
- No cardiovascular risk.
- Provides contraception for perimenopausal women who still need it.
- Convenient: "Set it and forget it".
- Has been shown to reduce the risk of uterine cancer as well as cervical and ovarian cancer.

The bad side:
- The IUD must be inserted, and although usually this involves minimal discomfort, for some women it is more difficult.
- Some women will experience spotting or bleeding, particularly in the beginning.
- Though rare, occasionally women will experience side effects, such as moodiness, fatigue, and bloating. These generally dissipate with time.
- It has not been established how long endometrial protection will be in effect, because in clinical trials, only contraceptive effectiveness, not uterine protection effectiveness, was studied. Most clinicians use the higher amount of hormone found in Mirena™ and Liletta™.
- The IUD must be replaced as long as estrogen therapy is continued. Most clinicians replace the IUD every seven years, but this is not based on good data.
- An IUD that is placed post-menopause is not covered by insurance.

A Period Post Menopause?

Some protocols for using post-menopause hormone therapy are cyclic, meaning that an estrogen and progestogen combination is not taken every single day. If hormone therapy is taken cyclically, it is not unusual to bleed on the days when the estrogen/progestogen combination, or a progestogen, is not taken.

This is sometimes a useful approach when a woman is perimenopausal and still menstruating, but it is in no way medically beneficial once someone has entered menopause. The exception is the woman who does not tolerate a progestogen and is placed on a protocol where she only uses it two weeks out of the month. Then there is the woman who wants to get a period because she thinks it is more "natural." I have not met that woman, but I have heard about her. News flash: It is not more natural. There is nothing natural about post-menopause hormone therapy.

There is NO medical benefit to having a period post-menopause.

Bleeding on Continuous Therapy

What if you are using hormone therapy on a daily, continuous basis and begin to spot or bleed heavily enough that a pad or tampon is required? First, don't panic! Of course, it is always disconcerting to have unexpected vaginal bleeding, and it's particularly unsettling when it occurs years after your uterus and ovaries have closed for business. It's not just about making the midnight run for sanitary products; it's that stomach-dropping fear that "blood equals cancer" that causes women to spend hours searching the internet for reassurance. Even though most women imagine the worst, in most cases, post-menopausal bleeding is not an indication of anything serious.

Keep in mind that though blood on the toilet paper can be coming from the vagina, rectum, or bladder, and though it seems as if the source should be obvious, it's not always easy to know. When in doubt, put in a tampon (you may have to borrow one from your daughter). If the tampon stays white but there is blood in the toilet bowl, it's most likely coming from the rectum or bladder and has nothing to do with your hormone therapy. A visit to your primary care doctor is in order.

If the blood is coming from your vagina and you have just started hormone therapy and the bleeding is very light, it is generally OK to wait a bit and see if it goes away.

But if it is persistent or heavy, it must be checked out. Most abnormal bleeding is not an indication of uterine cancer, but it should never be ignored. In many cases, all that is needed is an adjustment of your hormone therapy dosage.

Tempting, But Not Recommended

Many of my patients ask if it is OK to take estrogen without a progestogen. Giving estrogen without something to balance it out to prevent an abnormal buildup in the lining of the uterus is known as taking unopposed estrogen. Although it can be done very short term, the increased risk of uterine cancer is significant enough that it should not be done for the long term. The exception may be a woman who is taking a low dose of estrogen and is willing to periodically get ultrasounds to make sure there is no abnormal buildup. This approach is not currently recommended, but in the future, it may be a reasonable alternative for women at low risk of uterine cancer.

What about taking a progestogen less often? Some women are given the green light to take a progestin only for 14 days every three months. This protocol may not offer adequate uterine protection.

The vaginal progestin gels used in the fertility world to stabilize the uterine lining during early pregnancy are also sometimes prescribed for post-menopause women who do not tolerate oral progestins, but they have not been tested in post-menopausal women. It is unknown whether they provide adequate uterine protection.

Compounded progesterone or yam creams are not protective. The details are covered in the next chapter.

Although it sounds drastic, some of my patients have opted to have their uterus removed and take estrogen alone rather than deal with the risks and side effects of progestins. Generally, that is not a solution unless you have another good reason to have your uterus removed.

FRANCEY RECALLS that Dr. Herpes mentioned something about an IUD if the progesterone doesn't sit well with her. That seems like a good alternative, particularly after doing her internet research and learning that a progestogen IUD was Angelina Jolie's approach after she had her ovaries removed at age 39 to prevent ovarian cancer. Good enough for an actress, good enough for her.

14

ESTROGEN IS NOT POISON

Only 7% of women with hot flashes ultimately accept a prescription for estrogen.

The Flush Heard Round the World

JULY 2, 2002 the results of the Women's Health Initiative (WHI) were released. Millions of women turned on the news to hear that the estrogen, they took every morning could cause breast cancer, heart disease, blood clots, and stroke. The news immediately went viral, and women were advised that the hormone therapy their doctors had recommended was in fact dangerous and should be discontinued *immediately*.

There was a collective national flush as understandably nervous, angry women tossed their hormones down the toilet.

JULY 2, 2002

Bad news for women, but good news for my media career, which took off after I appeared on virtually every TV channel discussing the results. My take away was that not every woman was a candidate for estrogen and to always keep makeup at the office, just in case.

Prescriptions dropped by 70%.

The Women's Health Initiative Study (WHI)

It was medically accepted that estrogen would alleviate hot flashes. The WHI was a large study initiated in 1997 with the purpose of definitively determining whether long-term hormone therapy could also prevent heart disease and prolong life in addition to controlling post-menopausal symptoms.

Twenty-seven thousand women between the ages of 50 and 79 were divided into three groups.

Group 1 took oral estrogen and progestin.

Group 2 took only oral estrogen (women who had had a hysterectomy and did not need a progestin).

Group 3 was given a placebo (no hormone) pill.

The women were not told what they were taking, and they were all monitored for side effects and potential benefits. The study was intended to run for eight years but was abruptly ended at five years when it appeared that the group taking estrogen and progestin had a higher incidence of breast cancer, blood clots, and stroke than the placebo group.

Understanding and Putting the WHI in Perspective

Most media outlets that blared the negative news about hormone therapy forgot to emphasize that 97.5% of women taking estrogen and progestin therapy had no problems, and the number of women who had complications was actually quite small.

Specifically, the WHI showed that for **every 10,000** women per year who used estrogen and progestin (compared to the women who were not taking any hormones or were taking estrogen alone), there were:

Seven additional myocardial infarctions
Eight additional strokes
Eight additional breast cancers
Eight additional pulmonary embolisms
Six fewer colorectal cancers
Five fewer hip fractures
ZERO additional deaths

Since the initial release of the WHI findings in 2002, the data has been revisited, and it is now clear that both the design of the study and the initial interpretation of the data were problematic. There were three main issues:
- The age and characteristics of the women in the study.
- The type of progestin the study participants received.
- That only oral estrogen was studied.

Issue #1: Age and Timing of Therapy Matters
The average age of women in the WHI was 63, and over 70% of the women enrolled were over the age of 60. Because most women go through menopause between the ages of 50 and 55 (representing only 10% of the study population), the overall results were not reflective of most women who take hormone therapy. The main reason the women in the study were older is that only women who were no longer having hot flashes were eligible because the researchers did not want women to know if they were getting a placebo drug or actual hormones. So not only did the results reflect the consequences of aging, but they also included any possible damage the women might have experienced from having hot flashes prior to enrolling in the WHI.

A reevaluation of the study looking only at women in the 50- to 60-year-old range showed completely different and very reassuring results, including a decrease in coronary heart disease and a decrease in overall mortality.

> *There is a "critical window" to start hormone therapy to decrease cardiovascular risk and promote longevity.*

In addition to age and timing, the cardiovascular data was limited by the fact that the WHI did not identify who was taking statin drugs and who was not. In a subsequent Swedish study, 40,000 women took statins along with beta estradiol, and 38,000 did not. Over four years, the number of deaths and cardiovascular events, such as heart attack and stroke, were recorded. The rate of death from any cause was 33 each year for every 10,000 women who used hormone therapy with statins compared with 87 each year for every 10,000 women who used statins alone—a significant difference.

Women With Early or Premature Menopause **Were Not Included**

It's important to note that the WHI study did not include any women under the age of 50. Young women who have gone through an early or premature menopause are usually lumped together with the over-50 crowd. As a result, the 36-year-old who takes hormone therapy feels she is putting herself at the same risk, and has the same issues, as the 65-year-old who takes hormone therapy. No one worries about a 36-year-old woman taking birth control pills, but if the same woman goes through menopause, many erroneously believe that her taking estrogen therapy (which provides dramatically less of the hormone than in a typical pill) is dangerous.

Along those lines, it's interesting to me when I have a patient who is sailing through perimenopause on her birth control pill but balks when I tell her it is time to stop the pill and suggest menopausal hormone therapy. When I point out that the synthetic, non-bioidentical pill she has been happily taking for the last 20 years has a far greater potency of estrogen than standard post-menopausal hormone therapy, she is usually shocked.

Issue #2: **The Progestin Problem**

Many women were also unaware that the results released in 2002 applied only to women taking estrogen and a progestin. The WHI study group that included women who took estrogen alone was not discontinued until March 2004 and had strikingly different results.

Women in the 50- to 60-year-old WHI group who took estrogen alone had a:

- 37% *decrease* in heart disease.
- 11% *decrease* in stroke.
- 12% *decrease* in new-onset diabetes.

- 30% *decrease* in fractures.
- **18% *decrease* in breast cancer.**

You read that right.

The news flash that didn't make it to the media was that in the estrogen-only group, there was an 18% decrease in breast cancer.

It is now clear that the modest increase that is sometimes seen in breast cancer in women who take hormone therapy is due to the *progestin, not the estrogen.*

Blood clots were a concern. Blood clots that form in the veins of the legs can travel through the body and block blood vessels that supply the heart, lungs, or brain. The 50- to 60-year-old group in the WHI had a 37% increase in venous blood clots, which sounds alarming. Keep in mind, though, that because the number of blood clots occurring in that age group is very small, even a small increase translates into a huge percentage increase. In absolute numbers, there were four additional blood clots per 10,000 women per year of estrogen therapy.

It's also important to keep in mind that anyone can get a blood clot or develop heart disease even if they are not using hormone therapy. The risk of a clot is far greater in women who are obese and have high blood pressure and high cholesterol than in women who use post-menopause estrogen.

Overall, total mortality in the 50- to 59-year-old estrogen-only group was 30% lower than in women who did not take hormone therapy.

Although results for the estrogen-only group were very reassuring, there was essentially no media attention. I waxed my eyebrows in preparation to explain the good news on TV for nothing.

Summary for Ages 50 to 59, or Less Than 10 Years Since Menopause

Benefits of taking oral estrogen alone
Decrease in fractures
Decrease in diabetes
Decrease in breast cancer
Decrease in coronary artery disease
Decrease in overall mortality

Risks of taking oral estrogen alone
Increase in blood clots
Increase in stroke
Increase in gall stones

Benefits of taking oral estrogen plus progestin
Decrease in fractures
Decrease in diabetes
Decrease in coronary artery disease (but not as much as in the estrogen-only group)
Decrease in uterine cancer
Decrease in colorectal cancer
Decrease in overall mortality

Risks of taking oral estrogen plus progestin
Slight increase in lung cancer
Increase in breast cancer
Increase in blood clots
Increase in stroke
Increase in gall stones

Issue #3: Transdermal vs. Oral Estrogen: There Is a Difference

The third issue with the WHI was that it studied only one kind of hormone therapy. Having read chapter 12, you now know that transdermal estrogen therapy is significantly safer and does not have the serious risks of oral estrogen. Chapter 13 explains why medroxyprogesterone acetate is the problem when it comes to progestins. The WHI studied only oral Premarin™ (conjugated equine estrogen) and Provera™ (medroxyprogesterone acetate).

In 2012, the Kronos Early Estrogen Prevention Study (KEEPS) addressed some of the issues that were problematic in the WHI and compared transdermal to oral estrogen in addition to specifically including only women who were newly menopausal.

I'll give you the headline first: **Transdermal estrogen therapy, even with an oral progestin, if started soon after menopause not only relieved symptoms, but also was dramatically safer than oral estrogen.**

The Specifics

KEEPS was a four-year, randomized, double-blinded, placebo-controlled clinical trial (in other words: reliable, scientific, and unbiased) of low-dose oral or transdermal estrogen and progestin in 727 healthy women ages 42 to 58 who were within three years of the onset of menopause.

There were three groups.

- **Group 1** received oral estrogen (given as Premarin® 0.45 mg/day, a lower dose than the 0.625 mg/day used in the WHI) and MPA.
- **Group 2** received a transdermal estradiol (given as the Climara® patch 50 µg/day [µg = microgram]) and MPA.
- **Group 3** received a placebo (no hormone).

The women who used either oral or transdermal estrogen experienced excellent relief of their symptoms. There was no increase in their blood pressure, no effects on atherosclerosis, no increase in breast cancer or uterine cancer, and, most important, no increase in blood clots, stroke, or myocardial infarction (heart attacks). Transdermal estrogen did not affect cholesterol or triglycerides, and it lowered insulin resistance.

Though most women of average risk are safely able to take either an oral or transdermal estrogen if started soon after menopause, women who are at increased risk for blood clots, stroke, or heart disease should stick to a transdermal product.

Women with the following risk factors should avoid taking an oral estrogen:
- Prior history of a blood clot.
- Hereditary risk of blood clots (prothrombotic mutations).
- Obesity.
- High blood pressure.
- Diabetes.
- Elevated cholesterol and/or triglycerides.
- Liver disease.
- Gallbladder disease.
- Metabolic syndrome.
- Smoking habit.
- Initiation of therapy older than age 60.

Estrogen and the Breast Cancer Myth
The number one reason women avoid estrogen is not because of blood clots, but because of fear of breast cancer. Whenever someone is diagnosed with breast cancer, the first question often asked is, did she take hormone therapy? Not only does this perpetuate the myth that HT caused the breast cancer, but it validates women who have chosen not to.

Estrogen does not cause breast cancer. Period.

This is the one that will have a lot of you shaking your heads and thinking, "Is she kidding?" or "Is she stupid?" This is not my opinion. The facts speak for themselves.

- Over 80% of women who have breast cancer have never taken hormones.
- In the WHI study, only the women who took estrogen *and medroxyprogesterone acetate* together had a slight increase in breast cancer.
- The estrogen-only group had an 18% *decrease* in breast cancer.

Even if you consider the estrogen and progestin group who did have an increase in breast cancer, it was an extremely small risk: There were only **eight** *additional breast cancers for every 10,000 women who took HT.*

It is noteworthy that hormone therapy has essentially the same relative risk as drinking and being overweight and is less risky than delaying a first pregnancy. And when was the last time you heard of someone avoiding wine out of a fear of breast cancer?

Comparison of Relative Risks Contributing to Breast Cancer

Post-menopause obesity	1.2
Alcohol use	1.2
HORMONE THERAPY (estrogen and progestin)	1.3
Early menarche (first menstrual period)	1.3
Late menopause	1.5

Close relative with breast cancer younger than 50	1.8
Late first pregnancy	1.9
Dense breasts on mammogram	6.0
BRCA gene mutation	200

And if you still have doubts about the estrogen-and-breast-cancer connection, there is currently a multicenter clinical trial (The Promise Study) in which women with breast ductal carcinoma in situ are receiving a combination of conjugated equine estrogen and bazodoxifene to determine if this form of HT will prevent DCIS from progressing to invasive breast cancer. Perhaps knowing that a nationwide group of academic breast surgeons are intentionally giving patients who have been diagnosed with an early form of breast cancer estrogen will convince you that estrogen does not cause breast cancer.

Cognitive Function
The initial news from the WHI in the analysis of cognitive function was not reassuring. Data from WHIMS, the WHI Memory Study, showed a *decline* in memory and cognitive function in both the estrogen and the estrogen-progestin group compared to placebo. But every single woman in the WHIMS group was over the age of 65, and just as there appears to be a "critical window" to prevent cardiovascular disease, the same holds true when it comes to cognitive function. In the Kronos Early Estrogen Prevention Study (KEEPS), younger women receiving HT did not show a decline in memory or cognitive function.

Key Points:

- *The best time to start HT is at the onset of menopause.*

- *The type and route of estrogen make a difference.*

- *Women at risk for heart disease who take HT may benefit from taking a statin as well.*

The Fallout from the WHI Continues

Use of hormone therapy post-WHI dropped quickly, with only 2.8% of newly menopausal women signing on. And here we are 20 years later. Millions of women are suffering with hot flashes, vaginal dryness, and insomnia, and millions of women are at increased risk of cardiovascular disease, osteoporosis, and diabetes, because of the belief, propagated by the media and many doctors, that they are putting themselves at significant risk if they take hormone therapy. Although the number of women who use HT is currently higher than immediately post-WHI (somewhere in the neighborhood of 7%), accurate statistics of how many women use HT is difficult to come by because of the large numbers of undocumented prescriptions written for non-FDA-approved compounded HT.

The repercussions go far beyond women feeling miserable. A Yale study published in July 2013 suggested that continued false information in the media and concerns about estrogen have caused thousands of needless deaths. The authors estimated that up to 48,835 fewer women would have died between 2002 and 2012 if they had not avoided estrogen between the ages of 50 and 60. In another analysis, the decline in the use of estrogen-only therapy over 13 years was associated with a $4.1 billion increase in costs for treatment of chronic diseases such as breast cancer, coronary heart disease, colon cancer, and fractures among women in their 50s that could have been prevented had they taken HT.

It is also worth noting that the WHI did not evaluate quality of life, libido, or sexuality. And that counts for a lot.

Today: Why Women Don't Take Hormone Therapy

Most women are not offered treatment, and when they are, they more often than not decline based on:
- Lack of awareness about the impact of hot flashes.
- Misconceptions about the length of time symptoms will last.
- Confusion about the safety and efficacy of hormone therapy.

In a 2018 Gallop poll, only 3 in 5 women stated their doctor had discussed symptoms of menopause with them, and only 50% of those women were offered HT.

Even when prescribed, 35% decided not to take it due to concerns about side effects and cancer.

So although the subsequent reinterpretation of the WHI results is very reassuring, most women (and, sadly, too many doctors) are not aware that low-dose post-menopausal hormone therapy is appropriate and safe for most, if not all, women. Results from the WHI study have continued to contribute to the confusion and belief that hormone therapy is dangerous and, if taken, should be at the smallest dose for the shortest amount of time.

The dire warnings on the insert of every single estrogen product don't help. Evidently, the FDA did not get the memo about the safety of transdermals.

As mentioned in chapter 12, FDA class labeling requires all products containing the same ingredient to have the same warning, even if the risks have never been demonstrated in that product. The current FDA label reflects the original concerns about oral estrogen and progestin in older women. Yet, you will find the same FDA warnings on *every single estrogen product* whether it is oral, transdermal, or a local vaginal estrogen intended to treat vaginal dryness and painful intercourse.

Confusing, Misleading, and Incorrect FDA Warnings
"ESTROGENS INCREASE THE RISK OF ENDOMETRIAL CANCER"

This is true, but only if a woman does not use a progestogen or progestogen substitute to protect the uterine lining. Women that take estrogen and a progestogen have a lower risk of uterine cancer than women who do not use HT. In addition, it has been proven that endometrial cancer is not increased in for women using long term local vaginal estrogen.

"The Women's Health Initiative (WHI) study reported increased risks of myocardial infarction, stroke, invasive breast cancer, pulmonary emboli, and deep vein thrombosis in postmenopausal women (50 to 79 years of age) during 5 years of treatment with oral conjugated equine estrogens (CE 0.625 mg) combined with medroxyprogesterone acetate (MPA 2.5 mg) relative to placebo."

There is no mention that this was not seen in the estrogen only group, (other than blood clots), in the group aged 50-60, or in women who use transdermal products. This has never been shown to be true for women using a local vaginal estrogen.

"The Women's Health Initiative Memory Study (WHIMS), a substudy of WHI, reported increased risk of developing probable dementia in postmenopausal women 65 years of age or older during 4 years of treatment with oral conjugated equine estrogens plus medroxyprogesterone acetate relative to placebo."

This is true but there is no mention that this was not the case in women who started HT within ten years of the menopause transition. This has never been shown to be true for women using a local vaginal estrogen.

"Other doses of oral conjugated estrogens with medroxyprogesterone acetate, and other combinations and dosage forms of estrogens and progestins were not studied in the WHI clinical trials and, in the absence of comparable data, these risks should be assumed to be similar."

It is true that the WHI only studied oral conjugated estrogens and medroxyprogesterone acetate. It is not true that there is no comparable data. There is an abundance of data that proves that different formulas and different routes of delivery are safer.

"Because of these risks, estrogens with or without progestins should be prescribed at the lowest effective doses and for the shortest duration consistent with treatment goals and risks for the individual woman."

There is NO data to support this statement. And this has never been shown to be true for women using a local vaginal estrogen.

DURING THEIR NOW-WEEKLY Monday night martinis, Marla confesses that she too has abandoned yoga for hormone therapy. She, however, has ditched her gynecologist to go to a "hormone doctor," who customizes her hormone therapy and prescribes only "natural" hormones that are safer and better than the "poison" you get at the pharmacy. She must have read her mind because Francey has now carefully read the package insert, and she is terrified to start her new HT. Not to mention, she isn't exactly excited about having an IUD put in her uterus. Francey figures it is worth a consultation.

Francey scores an appointment with Marla's hormone specialist right away.

The receptionist tells her to cease her current estrogen regimen before her pre-consultation bloodwork. One week later, she stops by the office on her lunch break and leaves minus five tubes of blood and $2,500.

15

COMPOUNDED HORMONE THERAPY: BUYER BEWARE

LIKE MANY PHRASES, "bioidentical" means different things to different people. Generally, however, most women seeking "bioidentical hormones" are referring to compounded hormones as opposed to FDA-approved bioidentical hormone therapy distributed by commercial pharmaceutical companies.

Compounding Is Not a New Thing

Historically, all pharmacists compounded. In the 1800s, a doctor would give his patient a prescription to take to the local pharmacist, who would then mix the drug up per the doctor's specifications. As large commercial pharmaceutical companies came on the scene in the 1950s, compounding became the exception, not the rule, and was used only for products that were not commercially available.

The custom-compounded bioidentical industry took on an entirely different role when it began marketing and distributing so-called bioidentical hormones. In fact, "bioidentical" is not a scientific term. It is a term originally made up by savvy market-research gurus to describe hormones distributed by compounding pharmacies.

The use of the word "bioidentical" was brilliant. It was catchy, it sounded "natural," and it also sounded like something different than the duplicate FDA-approved plant-derived hormones produced and distributed by commercial pharmacies. And it worked. A multibillion-dollar industry was launched by an actress (more on that later) and supported by women desperate to feel better whose doctors were not helping them.

Though women generally distrust the pharmaceutical industry—which is legally obligated to back up its claims, do testing, and report all safety risks and negative findings—the general population seems to have little problem placing its trust in companies subject to no such efficacy or safety standards. This combined with aggressive marketing has resulted in women believing that compounded products are safer than standard products.

As a result, according to a 2015 North American Menopause Society (NAMS) survey, roughly 1 in 3 women who use hormone therapy obtain non-FDA-approved products from a compounding pharmacy. Most survey respondents were unaware that compounded hormones had not been evaluated or approved by the FDA. Most were unaware that compounded hormones have risks in addition to benefits.

Though there are manufacturing and quality-control issues at some, but not all, compounding pharmacies, in truth, the *prescribers* of compounded hormones are more of a problem than the actual compounded products. The *prescribers* of these products are the ones who misrepresent the benefits, don't discuss potential risks, and all too often manage hormones inappropriately.

DR. KASH IS DELIGHTFUL—and so encouraging! She sits with Francey for almost an hour, goes through all her lab results (there were pages), and talks about hormones Francey has never heard of, such as DHEA, estriol, and estrone. This person is clearly more knowledgeable than Dr. Herpes, who had only mentioned estrogen and progesterone, Francey thinks. Relieved to be in the hands of a real expert, she leaves with a prescription for custom compounded (based on her bloodwork) transdermal estrogen, testosterone, and progesterone— all conveniently in one cream to be applied to her thigh.

Prescribers of compounded bioidentical hormones often claim that these products reverse aging, enhance sex, and prevent cancer but, unlike FDA-approved commercial hormones, have no risks or side effects. It all sounds pretty good. But as with most things that sound too good to be true, it's important to separate the facts from the myths.

So let's look at the most common misconceptions I hear when it comes to compounded hormone therapy.

Misconception #1
Only compounded hormones are "natural."

The word "natural" means "as found in nature." Every single plant-derived estrogen product requires a multi-step chemical process to extract and convert estrogen precursors from a plant source into an estrogen powder that can then be put into a cream, a spray, a patch, or a pill. Every plant-derived hormone preparation, whether it comes from a compounding pharmacy or a large commercial pharmacy, is *synthesized*. The *only* thing that is truly natural is to eat the plant or drink the urine.

Promoters of compounded, plant-derived hormones use the terms "natural" and "bioidentical" because they are appealing to consumers and imply an advantage over manufactured pharmaceutical products. But "natural" does not equal "safer or better." We can all name many things that are natural but also unsafe. Arsenic, anthrax, and strychnine come to mind. And face it, what's more natural than *horse urine*? Humans are much closer to horses than plants.

Having said that, all FDA-approved plant-derived products from your corner drugstore are just as "natural" and "bioidentical" as the products you get from a compounding pharmacy.

Misconception #2
The estrogen in compounded hormones is different from the estrogen in commercial pharmaceutical products.

Compounding pharmacies don't manufacture hormones—they just mix them. Manufacturing factories extract estrogen precursors from plants, synthesize them to a useable form, and then sell the same active ingredients to both commercial pharmaceutical companies and compounding pharmacies. It's the same *stuff!* It all comes from the same place!

Think of it like sugar. Sugar is the active ingredient found in cookies, but before it can be used in a commercial product, it needs to be extracted from sugar cane, granulated, and then distributed to different cookie factories. Sugar can be mixed in different amounts with different ingredients to make different kinds of cookies. But the chemical makeup of sugar is the same in all cookies and has the same effect.

Misconception #3
Compounded hormones are safer than commercial hormones.

Because compounded alternatives to FDA-approved estrogen and progestogen formulations have the same active ingredient (see Misconception #2), they obviously are going to have the same benefits and the same safety concerns. But unlike the manufacturers of commercial hormones, the distributors and promoters of compounded hormones deny the known risks. And that's misleading. So how do they get away with it?

The FDA does not regulate compounded products, so there is no requirement for product labeling and no requirement for clinician or patient package inserts that document safety, side effects, and warnings. Instead, these prescribers tell women what women want to hear—namely, that compounded bioidentical hormones have fewer side effects and are more effective than identically structured, commercially produced hormones, even though there is no scientific evidence to prove that claim.

In addition, there are safety concerns unique to compounded products. They have not been tested in clinical trials to assure efficacy and safety, which means the recommended dosages, delivery systems, and protocols have never been shown to be safe, much less safer or more effective, than conventional prescription hormone products. The issue with compounded progesterone cream is a case in point (see Misconception #4).

Sticking with the cookie analogy, a cookie loaded with sugar can be sold by either Nabisco—where it is commercially prepared and packaged bearing a specific list of ingredients and a calorie count to let you know that if you eat a lot of cookies, you will get fat—or by the corner bakery, which puts no listing of ingredients on its box and is free to advertise that its cookies will not make you fat.

Misconception #4
Compounded progesterone will prevent uterine cancer.

After reading chapter 13, you appreciate the importance of protecting your uterus when taking estrogen therapy. When you finished the chapter, you might have wondered why progesterone cream was not on the list of approved products. The answer is, progesterone cream doesn't protect the uterus. Though compounding pharmacies and prescribers offer transdermal progesterone creams, to date no scientific studies have demonstrated that they protect the uterine lining from developing precancer or cancer. In fact, there is data to support just the opposite.

A 2015 survey published by the North American Menopause Society showed that in a group of 324 women, there were four cases of endometrial cancer in women using compounded hormone therapy compared to zero cases of endometrial cancer in the group using commercial products.

Biologically, it makes sense that these creams don't work. The molecule is poorly absorbed through the skin, and systemic progesterone levels simply never get high enough to protect the uterine lining. Using a compounded progesterone cream is essentially the equivalent of using nothing.

Misconception #5
Compounded hormones undergo the same quality
control as commercial products.

Compounding pharmacies don't manufacture hormones—they just mix them. The problem is that they sometimes don't mix them very accurately. In 2013, investigative
reporter Cathryn Ramin, on behalf of *More* magazine, com-
missioned lab tests of hormones distributed by 12 popular
compounding pharmacies and found that, despite identical prescriptions for estrogen and progesterone, there was
no uniformity in what was compounded. Virtually every
sample was either significantly lower than what was prescribed or significantly higher. There was even variation in
capsules from the same pharmacy. A woman who has been
prescribed 50 milligrams of estradiol might be taking 25
milligrams one day and 100 milligrams the next.

Lack of FDA oversight also means that quality is not en-
sured in drugs from compounding pharmacies. The public became acutely aware of this in 2012, when 749 people
became ill and 63 of them died of meningitis after a compounding pharmacy in Massachusetts manufactured and
distributed contaminated steroids. In 2013, the FDA conducted 31 unannounced inspections in 18 states of other
compounding pharmacies and found rust and mold in
"clean" areas along with tears in workers' gloves. Unsterile
and potentially risky conditions were found in all but one
of the inspected compounding manufacturing plants.

A 2001 study looked at 29 products from 12 compounding pharmacies and found that 34% of the products tested
failed quality-control measures versus 2% of commercially manufactured drug products, and 25% failed potency
standards.

Do most compounding pharmacies do a terrific job in maintaining quality and consistency? Of course. You just can't count on it the same way you can with a commercial enterprise. Many commercial pharmacies, such as CVS and Walgreens, also compound, which assures quality control, purity of the product, and consistency of dosages.

Misconception #6
Compounded HT is customized based on your hormone levels.

Compounding prescribers promote the idea that their bioidentical hormones are customized for each individual patient. Sometimes this customization is based on saliva tests, even though it has been scientifically proven that salivary levels are affected by diet and other variables. Likewise, blood tests, though more accurate, are not routinely used to determine the appropriate dosage of hormone therapy because there is a wide range of "normal," and serum levels do not correspond to efficacy. What matters is not a target number but how someone feels.

Frequent testing gets you in the door on a regular basis, and is very lucrative for prescribers, but it makes it appear that you are getting something made to order just for you. I point out to my patients that virtually everyone that comes to me with their "personally compounded hormone therapy" has pretty much the exact same formula that is rarely altered based on bloodwork. In truth, compounded hormones are now almost never customized. Some compounding pharmacies mass-produce hormone preparations that are almost exact copies of those produced commercially.

Misconception #7
Big Pharma is only in it for the money.

Of course Big Pharma is in it for the money! This is America. And that is what the FDA is for: to make sure greed does not get in the way of patients getting safe, effective drugs. The compounding pharmacies are *just* as profit-motivated, except no one is regulating or overseeing them. Compounded hormones are now a multibillion-dollar-a-year industry. Many physicians who prescribe from compounding pharmacies require large amounts of expensive tests that are not covered by insurance. Compounded hormones are rarely covered by insurance. No expensive clinical trials or testing is required to bring the product to market. Let's just be clear about who is in it for the money.

Misconception #8
Prescribers of compounded hormones are hormone experts.

This is the one that makes my blood boil. Our first expert is "Dr." Suzanne Somers, as in Suzanne Somers, the *actress*, who was the main driver popularizing the compounding industry when she published her best-selling 2007 book, *"Ageless: The Naked Truth About Bioidentical Hormones."*

Somers admits that she is "not an expert," which is obvious seeing as she has no education or credentials to back up her medical claims. But as a self-proclaimed nonexpert, it is kind of interesting how she doles out advice and opinions that she presents as facts. In *Ageless* (which still sells well), she relies on her cadre of so-called "real" experts.

Her number one expert is T. S. Wiley, a high school graduate who wrote her own book, appropriately called *Sex, Lies and Menopause.* Not only does Wiley rationalize the use of compounded hormone therapy, but she also pro-motes specific protocols for how it should be given. She invented the Wiley protocol, a high-dose regimen of cyclic hormone therapy (meaning that even 80-year-old women get periods) that will "prevent cancer" and maintain youth into one's 90s. All of this is based on Wiley's theory that be-cause 30-year-old women don't get cancer, if you maintain hormones like a 30-year-old, you won't get cancer. Huh? Her education when she wrote all of this? She didn't quite make it to medical school. In fact, she didn't make it past her first year of college.

In addition, none of the doctors in *Ageless* who are pre-sented as authorities in the field of hormones and meno-pause would be considered experts by any academic insti-tution or knowledgeable physicians. The majority are not board certified in anything. None have been published in the scientific literature. Most don't have hospital affilia-tions. The few who are board certified are not in gynecology or endocrinology but, inexplicably, in emergency medicine. I have spent enough time in ERs to tell you that even women with the worst cases of hot flashes and vaginal dryness do not go to the Emergency Department, so it is a mystery to me how these doctors are such experts. I know all of this because prior to appearing on *The Oprah Winfrey Show* with Suzanne Somers, I read every sentence in *The Sexy Years* (it was painful) and researched every "expert" in the book.

Feel free to visit DrStreicher.com to watch the video of me and Suzanne duking it out on 20/20 and then again on *The Oprah Winfrey Show*. But that's a whole other story.

Ageless aside, most of the longevity and hormone "experts" who prescribe compounded hormones and have made a fortune in the highly lucrative hormone business are from a variety of unrelated specialties. Many of these docs are "board certified" in "antiaging," which, despite a very official and impressive looking diploma, is not a certification recognized by the American Board of Medical Specialties. Doctors who make a living from prescribing compounded HT often never take your complete history, never have you get undressed, never do an examination, and never deal with complications. I cannot tell you how many times a woman seeing one of these "hormone experts" is referred to an actual gynecologist when she starts to bleed.

For what it's worth, the real experts that comprise medical societies, including the American Association of Clinical Endocrinologists, the American Congress of Obstetricians and Gynecologists, the American Medical Association, the American Society for Reproductive Medicine, the Endocrine Society, the North American Menopause Society, the U.S. Preventive Services Task Force, and the American College of Clinical Pharmacy, all caution against the use of compounded hormone therapy. Check out chapter 17 for more on how to find an expert.

OK, I'm done ranting.

A Chip in the Hip?

An increasing number of women who choose compounded hormones end up with a hormone pellet under the skin of the hip that releases estrogen and testosterone and lasts four to six months. When a woman initially gets a pellet, she always feels great. There is nothing like a huge surge of estrogen and testosterone to ensure a great libido, no flashes, and tons of energy.

As with other compounded products, women are told that these hormones are safer and more effective than standard therapy. *What they are not told* is that this form of hormone therapy is completely unregulated. In the NAMS survey, 86% of respondents had no idea pellets were not FDA approved. Patients are also not told that pellets generally have sky-high doses of estrogen and testosterone, well above what any woman would produce at any time in her life.

A 2021 study published in the journal *Menopause* investigated 539 women using pellets compared to women using commercial hormone therapy.

The average peak serum estradiol level in the pellet group was 237.70 pg/mL, compared with 93.45 pg/mL—more than twice as high!

The average peak testosterone level was 192.84 ng/dL in pellet users versus 15.59 ng/dL. As a point of reference, a testosterone level of at least 300 ng/dL is normal for a man. Women generally are in the 8 ng/dL to 60 ng/dL range.

> *No wonder women who use pellets sometimes have an enlarged clitoris, experience male pattern baldness, and have to borrow their husband's razor and their teenager's acne cream.*

The study reported that, compared to women using FDA-approved hormone therapy, women using pellets were more likely to experience:
- Mood swings.
- Anxiety.
- Breast tenderness.

- Male pattern baldness.
- Acne.
- Weight gain.
- Abnormal bleeding.
- Hysterectomy.

Specifically, 55.3% of patients experienced abnormal uterine bleeding. During the 12 years of the study, 20.3% of pellet users had a hysterectomy, compared with 6.3% of the women using FDA-approved therapy.

Overall, 57.6% of the patients on pellet therapy had side effects versus 14.8% on standard therapy.

I see women in the clinic all the time who are looking for solutions to these side effects. Unfortunately, we have no choice but to wait it out because once in, the pellets can't be removed. Safer? Better? I don't think so.

More is not better; excessive levels do not demonstrate a greater efficacy, and these super-physiologic levels are more likely to have a negative impact due to side effects.

AFTER HEADING HOME from her appointment with Dr. Kash, Francey is a little nervous that the doctor never examined her, and although the diplomas hanging on the wall were impressive—and there were so many of them—it was a little weird that her specialty was emergency medicine.

Just to be cautious, she schedules another telehealth visit with Dr. Herpes (whom she realizes she does trust after all). The doctor says she is not interested in seeing Francey's $2,500 worth of hormone tests because she already knows that, like every menopausal woman, Francey's progesterone level is zero, and her estradiol level is nonexistent.

Do I Prescribe Compounded Hormones?

Absolutely. I routinely use a compounding pharmacy that I know and trust *when I need a product that is not available commercially*. But when it comes to bioidentical estrogen, progesterone, and other progestogens, there is no advantage to using a compounding pharmacy.

Most menopause and sexual health experts in this country prescribe and recommend FDA-approved bioidentical plant-derived estrogen, produced and distributed by companies that have quality-control standards and are obligated to tell you not only the benefits but the potential risks as well.

In summary:

- Compounded hormones have the same active ingredient as most commercially available hormones.
- *Prescribers* of compounded hormones are often more of an issue than the compounding pharmacies.
- There are unique safety concerns regarding compounded products because they are not regulated or monitored.
- There is no requirement for labeling to outline risks.
- Compounded hormones have no scientific efficacy and safety data.
- Compounded hormones have never been shown to be more effective than commercial hormone therapy.
- There is also no scientific basis to support the use of routine serum levels because there is a wide therapeutic window.
- Random checks have found that overdosing or underdosing is common seeing as there are inconsistencies from pharmacy to pharmacy—and even within the same pharmacy.

- For women with a uterus, there is an increased risk of inadequate endometrial protection and a greater likelihood of endometrial cancers.

I don't blame women who choose a prescriber of compounded hormones. Women are just looking for answers and too often their own doctors are not helping them. If qualified doctors were experts in hormone therapy and menopause, women would not turn to physician entrepreneurs who are taking advantage of women who are just trying to feel better.

And it's scary to think that millions of women are unwittingly using prescription hormones that have never gone through a new drug approval process to substantiate safety, prove efficacy, and ensure quality.

One last thing... commercially available products will likely be covered by insurance. The non-FDA-approved compounded versions will require you to open your checkbook as well as your trust.

FAST-FORWARD SIX MONTHS: Francey is flash-free, is sleeping, and has even taken off a few pounds.
Hot flash hell is history!
Thankfully, she has not been fired from her job, her insurance pays for her hormone therapy, and she is even thinking about going back to school to finish her degree. She smiles and thinks that maybe she will even go out with out with the guy from the marketing department who she is pretty sure has been flirting with her. Life is good. WHAT COULD POSSIBLY GO WRONG...

THE SAGA OF FRANCEY'S JOURNEY through menopause
continues!

Dr. Streicher's Inside Information Series
Slip Sliding Away: Turning Back the Clock on Your Vagina

**Hot Flash Hell: A Gynecologists Guide to Turning Down
the Heat**

Coming Soon!
**Put the O Back into Mojo: A Post Menopause Guide to
Orgasm**

Menopause and the Itchy Vulva

**Men on Pause: A Gynecologists Guide for Men About
Women**

Reclaiming Lost Libido Post Menopause

Incontinence-Say No! To Diapers

Dating After 50: Inside Information from a Gynecologist

Cancer, Menopause and Feeling Fabulous

Part 3
INSIDE INFORMATION
RESOURCES

16

CALLING DR. GOOGLE?

I GET IT. Why take off work, sit in someone's waiting room, pay a fee, and have a potentially painful and/or humiliating exam just to get a diagnosis you can get in the privacy of your own home, fully dressed, at any hour, from a source that does not require stirrups, speculums, or insurance?

According to the Pew Research Center, eighty percent of internet users consult it for pretty much everything that ails them in lieu of seeing a doctor. There are 40,000 health-related searches on Google *every second*, which translates to over 3.5 billion health searches per day.

Here's the Problem
When you (or someone you know) has received a diagnosis or has a symptom and are looking for information, the internet can be a good thing. On the other hand, the information could be misleading, wrong, and/or terrifying.

Google HPV (a very common search term) and you will learn that human papilloma virus is responsible for cervical, anal, vulvar, lung, and throat cancer. All terrifyingly true, but the majority of women with a diagnosis of HPV on their Pap test need no treatment. In most cases, the body clears the virus, and a follow-up Pap is all that is required. The overwhelming majority of women do not get cancer.

But human nature being what it is, most women will assume the worst, panic, become anxious, and, in many cases, with the tap of a link, buy one of the many worthless "miracle cures" that just happen to pop up on the same site that answers your questions about HPV.

Be Your Own Doctor!

Self-diagnosis based on an internet search of symptoms is also dangerous. Studies have shown that only thirty-five percent of adults follow up with a physician. Most assume they have something more serious than they actually have.

Eighty percent of adults Google their symptoms before a doctor or emergency department visit. One study that surveyed adults in an ER found that almost all had looked up their symptoms and arrived having "self-diagnosed" their condition. Only twenty-nine percent left the emergency department with their perceived diagnosis confirmed.

What's Good About Using the Internet for Health Info

Very often, checking out symptoms online will get someone to a doctor. Good information can also keep someone from going to a doctor unnecessarily. And, yes, an informed patient is a really good thing. It makes my job much easier when I have a patient who has done her "homework" and knows a lot about her condition. The key is, she needs access to scientifically accurate information.

Getting Good Information

A lot of folks assume that if they are on a medical website, like WebMD, they are getting accurate information.

Sometimes that is the case, but you can't count on it. Occasionally, I do a search on WebMD and am horrified by the lack of information, the misinformation, or the out-of-date information.

Whether you are checking out symptoms to see if your headache is eyestrain or brain cancer or looking for potential side effects before you pop a pill, it would be nice to have some reassurance that the information you are reading is medically accurate.

Tips to Know **If a Site is Medically Accurate**

- **Look at who wrote the article.** A twenty-five-year-old freelance writer is not the best person to get information from on local vaginal estrogen, even if she supposedly interviewed experts. I have seen my own quotes taken out of context many times.
- **If an expert didn't write it, did an expert review it?** And is the "expert" really an expert? An MD after a name is not always a guarantee that he or she is an expert in that area.
- **When was it written?** Many sites avoid putting dates on their articles, and you have no way of knowing how current the information is.
- **Is the site sponsored?** If someone is trying to sell you something, beware.

My List of **Trustworthy Websites**

Although I recommend these websites as having information that is generally up to date and accurate, my endorsement doesn't mean I agree with everything on them (except for my own website, of course!).

DrStreicher.com

I wrote every word that appears on my site, and every article has been exhaustively researched. My site has articles on virtually every aspect of women's health. My favorite section includes my articles on the history of medicine. Though I do update, there may be the occasional article that needs refreshing.

UpToDate (www.uptodate.com)

This go-to site for physicians and other health care professionals requires a paid subscription, but there is also has a free patient portal. All articles were written not only by physicians, but by a top expert in that field. There are comprehensive articles on virtually every medical condition, including pediatrics. The information in the patient portal is understandable and, though written for consumers, not dumbed down. And the reason it is called UpToDate is that every article is reviewed and updated with new information every few months. In addition, there are links to relevant sites or articles for people who want more information.

Mayo Clinic (www.mayohealth.org)

This site is good for general medical information about specific symptoms, tests, and procedures. It is particularly useful when checking out a medication. There is information on both prescription and over-the-counter medications, including what a drug is made of what it does, precautions, and its side effects.

The National Center for Complementary and Integrative Medicine (www.nccih.nih.gov)

Instead of relying on the "expert" at the corner health food store, go to the National Center for Complementary and Integrative Medicine's website to find accurate, up-to-date

safety and efficacy information on specific herbs, supplements, and practices (such as acupuncture). You can also
look up specific conditions to learn alternative and complementary options.

The North America Menopause Society (www.menopause.org)
The North America Menopause Society's website is intended for health care clinicians, but it has loads of consumer information on menopause. More important, it is the
place to go to find a certified menopause practitioner.

And for those who really want to do a deep dive, head on
over to **PubMed** at https://www.ncbi.nlm.nih.gov/pubmed/
to delve into medical journals.

**Promises, Promises: A Word About Over-the-Counter
Products**
Scroll the web and you're likely to be bombarded by ads for
a plethora of products that promise to remove wrinkles,
tighten your vagina, cure incontinence, or ensure orgasmic
ecstasy. It's a wonder that anyone has anything but perfect
skin, a failproof bladder, and a fabulous sex life—at least
if you believe the testimonials that accompany these ads.

But in truth, most of these products haven't gone
through any kind of testing process to ensure that their
claims actually happen.

"How can that be," you ask, "when virtually all of
these devices and products have a U.S. Food and Drug
Administration seal?"

The answer is: An FDA-*listed* product doesn't equal an
FDA-*approved* product. Despite the reassuring blue FDA
logo, most over-the-counter products and devices are not
FDA approved. They're simply cleared, listed, or registered
by the FDA.

An FDA-approved drug goes through an extensive vetting process that not only ensures that it is safe, but also that it does what it says it will do. Prescription drugs are all FDA approved.

An FDA-cleared drug is a product that is sold over the counter. FDA-cleared drugs do not claim to cure a specific condition. As an example, a lubricant cannot say that it is used to treat genitourinary syndrome of menopause (a medical condition), but it can claim to "enhance intimacy." An FDA-cleared product does not go through the same approval process as an FDA-approved drug, and though it is likely to be safe, it may not necessarily do what it claims to do. In fact, most claims are simply an impressive triumph of marketing over science.

In the case of FDA-registered products, the company that makes a product, and its marketers, determine what language is used and, yes, what the product claims to do. No scientific studies are required, and no scientific studies are performed, because it's not in a company's best interest to do so. Why would a company spend millions of dollars on a study that might prove that its face cream doesn't actually eliminate wrinkles?

Similarly, the FDA doesn't regulate vitamins, herbs, or other dietary supplements, which is why so many of them claim to simply "promote" health as opposed to treating a specific illness.

17

FINDING A MENOPAUSE TEAM

ONCE YOU DO MAKE an appointment to see an actual doctor, how do you know that he or she can help you? I hear every day from women that when they went to their doctor with their dry giney woes they were told, "Buy a lube" Hot flashes? "Tough it out." End of story.

How is it that you're such an expert but your doctor may not be?

I hate to say this, but an "MD" after the name is no assurance that the person to whom you are about to bare your soul— and your vagina—is an expert in your problem.

Now that you are an expert, how do you find a health care practitioner who can help you navigate your way through menopause?

Sometimes the savvy consumer must do a little legwork to find a clinician who is a real expert on menopausal women. A menopause expert is not necessarily your gynecologist—or a gynecologist period. An expert is a medical professional who has an interest in this area and is informed about the diagnosis and treatment of the conditions that affect woman who are short on estrogen. So, a menopause expert might be your gynecologist, or an internist, or a family practice doctor. It's also possible that the best clinician to help you with your issue may not even be a doctor, but rather an advanced practice clinician.

I want to provide you with a quick and easy-to-understand guide to what you should look for when choosing a health care professional. If you understand who you are looking for, what kind of training is necessary for specific titles, how qualified a physician is, and how non-MD clinicians fit into the picture, you will have a better chance of getting the right treatment.

"Doctor": What's in a Title?

A "doctor" is anyone who has a doctorate-level degree. Anyone with "Doctor" in front of his or her name *might* be a physician, but might also be a dentist, podiatrist, psychologist, or English professor. If you are looking for a physician, look for an "MD."

MD *stands for "Medical Doctor." Anyone who has graduated from medical school is allowed to put "MD" after their name. Forever.* **DO** *stands for "Doctor of Osteopathy." An osteopath's training is essentially identical to an MD's and should be considered equivalent.*

Licensing

A licensed physician is a physician who is allowed to practice medicine. Each state has its own criteria for granting licenses, but in general, licensure to practice medicine requires only proof of graduation from medical school, at least a year of clinical training, and passing a qualifying exam. To verify that a physician is licensed, go to the Federation of State Medical Boards website (fsmb.org). Please note that licensure is not the same thing as board certification and does not guarantee expertise in a specific field.

Board Certification

Board certification is the gold standard that assures you that a physician is an expert in a specialty or subspecialty. The American Board of Medical Specialties (ABMS) is the medical organization that oversees physician certification by developing standards for the evaluation and certification of physician specialists. To be board-certified, a doctor must complete a residency (post-medical school training) in his or her specialty that has been recognized by ABMS, followed by rigorous written and oral examinations. If a doctor wants to subspecialize, he or she must then complete fellowship training after finishing residency. For example, to be a board-certified fertility specialist, a medical school graduate must complete a four-year residency in the obstetrics-gynecology specialty, followed by a three-year fellowship in the subspecialty of reproductive endocrinology and infertility.

If that wasn't enough, a specialist or subspecialist must maintain board certification by taking medical courses and passing tests to prove that he or she is up to date. The criterion in each field is specific to the specialty. Some, but not all, board-certified doctors designate their certification as part of their title. For example, a board-certified gynecologist with the letters FACOG after his or her name is a Fellow in the American College of Obstetricians and Gynecologists. ABMS.org is the site where you can check out whether a physician is board-certified and find out what he or she is certified in.

Board Certified in Anti-Aging?

By the way, "Anti-Aging" is not a specialty recognized by The American Board of Medical Specialties and does not require a residency. All that is required for certification from the American Board of Anti-aging and Regenerative Medicine is to complete a self-learning course, pass an examination and submit six patient charts for review by their board. According to their website, only five percent of physicians that have completed this course are gynecologists, which means that ninety-five of physicians that practice anti-aging are not experts when it comes to gynecologic exams or treatment of gynecologic issues. It also explains why so many of them prescribe hormones without ever having their patients take off their clothes.

University Affiliations

It's generally a good sign if a physician has an academic appointment at a medical school. Faculty ranks such as instructor, assistant professor, associate professor, and professor depend on physicians' level of involvement in teaching medical students, their research, and the number and stature of their publications.

If a doctor is not board-certified or has no university affiliation, does this mean he or she is a bad doctor? Of course not! Many non-board-certified physicians are excellent doctors who keep up with advancements in their fields and give very good care. Let's face it, though: if you needed brain surgery, would you go to the brain surgeon who's board-certified, teaches at a medical school, and is current with the field, or would you pick the brain surgeon who finished a residency but failed her boards, took off five years to be an artist, and then returned and has privileges at a hospital that was in such desperate need of a brain surgeon that it didn't require board certification?

By now, I'm sure you get the message.

But vaginal dryness and hot flashes aren't brain surgery. What you need is someone who has an interest in menopause and a knowledge base. Sometimes this expert is a physician, sometimes an internist, sometimes a gynecologist, sometimes a family practice doctor, and sometimes a physician's assistant or nurse-practitioner (more on them later). You may be thinking, *But I'm seeing an expert! If a gynecologist isn't an expert in this area, who is?*

Even in particular fields, doctors have areas of interest. A neurologist may be the world's expert on seizure disorders, but not know a lot about stroke. Your ob-gyn may have an incredible expertise about twin pregnancies and preterm labor but treats women with vaginal atrophy only a few times a year. So how do you know where a doctor's areas of interest lie?

Referral Services?

Most hospitals have a physician referral service and will help you find a doctor who is interested in and knowledgeable about your condition. If the hospital you have chosen is well known as a leader in women's health, then that hospital's referral service is usually a great way to find the right doctor. Keep in mind that the people who work in hospital referrals are obligated to make referrals to all the physicians on staff, so if you just call up and say, "Hi, I have a dry vagina. Which ob-gyn is good?" you'll most likely be given the name of whoever is next on the list.

You need to ask specific questions that will lead you to the doctor who is most appropriate for you. For example, instead of saying, "I need a gynecologist because sex hurts like hell," you might try, "I'm looking for a board-certified gynecologist who has been in practice for at least five years. I would prefer a woman and would like someone who takes care of a lot of menopausal problems and has identified herself as having an interest or expertise in sexual issues."

You can get a lot of information from physician referral, and it is well worth your time to tell the service exactly what's important to you in a doctor. The referral service will also be able to answer questions about office location and accepted insurance. Frequently, a referral service will help you get an appointment, even if you can't get one just by calling yourself.

Many hospitals also have a "physician finder" section on their website where you can type in a condition to find the physicians who list it as an area of expertise.

Hospital referral services are not the same as the commercial referral agencies that operate independently of hospitals. Take it from me—referral agencies that advertise in magazines, the yellow pages, or on TV are not a great source. Participating physicians pay to be part of the service and tell the service what to say. As with any paid advertisement, healthy skepticism is appropriate.

Searching Online for a Doctor

The reason for the increasing popularity of doctor-listing websites is that people are desperate for an easy way to find information about a doctor without making an appointment. In our digitally driven society, this seems to be a reasonable desire. After all, wouldn't someone who has already been to that doctor be the best judge of how approachable or knowledgeable he or she is?

Keep in mind that consumer referral lists are no better than asking strangers on the street what they think. Typically, there are no more than a handful of "reviewers" who are rating the doctors. The typical doctor sees thousands of patients a year, and the experience of two or three people is hardly reflective of a typical experience. More important, you have no idea who is writing these reviews or what their agenda is. A glowing review may be from the wife or mother of the doctor. A scathing review may be from a disgruntled patient or employee, or from the wife or mother of the competing doctor in town. It has become common for "online profile management" companies to post positive reviews for businesses and products for a fee.

Even if reviewers' comments accurately reflect their experience, their comments are usually more about how they were treated at the office than about the skills of the doctor.

More than one five-star comment has been posted because the doctor was "really friendly," "had a "great staff," and offered free estrogen samples.

Professional Societies

Professional societies such as the American Medical Association or the American College of Obstetricians and Gynecologists are all potential sources of referrals. But to find a menopause expert, your best bet is to head to the North American Menopause Society (NAMS) website, menopause.org.

North American Menopause Society

The mission of the North American Menopause Society (NAMS), a nonprofit scientific organization, is to promote the health and quality of life of all women during midlife and beyond through an understanding of menopause and healthy aging. To help meet its mission, NAMS developed a certification exam in 2002. Successful completion of the exam provides a doctor with a three-year credential as a NAMS Certified Menopause Practitioner (NCMP).

Menopausal medicine has become increasingly complex, so you are lucky if you find a doctor with this level of commitment and competence.

You can pretty much be guaranteed that a NAMS-certified practitioner has not only the interest but also the expertise to evaluate and treat any of your menopausal issues, including the sexual ones. To find a certified menopause practitioner, go to www.menopause.org.

Finding Non-MD Clinicians: Advanced Practice Nurses and Physician's Assistants

So, is an MD always the best clinician to help you deal with complex menopause issues? Sometimes a nonphysician is more qualified than many physicians when it comes to diagnosing and treating certain conditions. I am a huge advocate of advanced practice nurses (some are nurse-practitioners, and some have other advanced nursing degrees) and physician's assistants. In addition, an advanced practice nurse or physician's assistant is likely to spend more time with you than most physicians. I know this firsthand because I utilize invaluable advanced practice nurses and physician assistants in the Northwestern Medicine Center for Sexual Medicine and Menopause.

I made the decision to use the words "doctor" and "gynecologist" when referring to a clinician in this book because I am a gynecologist. Also, it would have been cumbersome to use "doctor and/or advanced practice clinician/physician's assistant" throughout the book. To add to the confusion, there are many different degrees that qualify a clinician as an advanced practice nurse.

What if Your Doctor Doesn't Have a Vagina?

Frequently, a new patient will say to me, "I've had the same ob-gyn for 20 years, and I love him, but he's a *man*, so of course there was no way I could talk to *him* about this! I want a woman doctor who will understand."

As a physician, I can tell you that I don't need to have personally experienced vaginal atrophy to help my patient with vaginal atrophy, any more than I need to experience a urinary tract infection to know how to treat it. The gender (and age!) of your clinician really shouldn't matter. *Really.* Obviously, if you are totally uncomfortable being examined by a man or talking to a man about intimate issues you will be better off with a woman doctor. If you feel somewhat guilty discriminating in this way, consider the number of men who go to women urologists. On the other hand, it would be foolish to go with the less qualified doctor based solely on gender, so keep an open mind.

Many women go to a woman gynecologist because they subconsciously—or even consciously—think that talking to a female gynecologist will be like talking to a girlfriend. While it is generally easier to talk to a girlfriend about menopause issues than to your doctor, you are not looking for a new friend at the doctor's office. You have plenty of people to invite to parties and have lunch with. When choosing your gynecologist, you are looking for someone who has the skills you need and whose judgment you trust. Your doctor need not be your friend, but she or he does need to be someone who will talk to you, listen to you, and help you. Sometimes that person is a woman, and sometimes it's a man.

Mention What You'd Like to Discuss When You Make Your Appointment

When you book the appointment, this is a good time to mention that you have an issue you would like to discuss. You can simply say, "In addition to my annual exam, I have some concerns related to pain during sex." It will then be noted as the reason for your visit, making it more likely that your doctor will bring up the issue. Some women find it easier to mention their concerns to the assistant who brings them into the examination room. The assistant lets the doctor know that the patient has brought up a specific topic, and then the doctor is likely to initiate the conversation.

Make a Separate Appointment

Often a patient will come for her annual "well woman" visit with multiple issues she wants to discuss. When I explain that there is not enough time to deal with all the problems in one visit and that another appointment needs to be made, sometimes I get an unhappy patient. I understand. You've taken time off from work, parked, and paid your copay. An additional visit is not only inconvenient but also expensive. But there simply isn't time to adequately address complex gynecological issues at the time of your annual exam, and they can't—and shouldn't—be quickly tagged onto your routine visit.

Many women are reluctant to make an additional appointment, since their insurance may cover only "well woman" visits and not "problem" visits. But face it, you are having a problem! You deserve and need more time. Your doctor is going to take the time to evaluate and treat the problem if that is specifically why you've made an appointment to see him or her. If it is important enough to you to mention the problem, give yourself permission to go for another appointment. Most initial visits in the Northwestern Medicine Center for Menopause last one hour. Most annual visits for a well woman exam allot fifteen minutes.

Consider Seeing a Menopause Specialist, **Even if Your Insurance Doesn't Cover It**

Even if you do your homework, you may simply not have access to a menopause expert. You may live in a small town, or your insurance may keep you locked into a particular group of physicians. While good health care is our right and I believe every man and woman should have access to a doctor who can help them, sometimes the care you need is not available within the limitations of your health care plan. If you really feel that you can't discuss your issues with your current doctor, or if your doctor seems truly clueless or embarrassed when you bring them up, bite the bullet and spend the money to see someone who can help you, even if that person is not covered by your insurance plan. Keep in mind that it is likely that you will need only one or two consultations. And you do not need to end your relationship with your regular gynecologist, whom you can continue to see for routine visits.

If All **Else Fails...**

If you have a hard time talking to your doctor about your issue and you don't have the option of seeing another practitioner, I hope that my Inside Information guides at least will have helped you identify your issues and given you ways to fix them. If you think you need to see a pelvic physical therapist, ask your doctor for a referral. If you need a prescription for a local estrogen, just ask for the one you want. Most likely, your doctor will just give you the referral and the pre- scription, no questions asked. You're welcome!

18

RESOURCES

ALTHOUGH I RECOMMEND these resources as containing information that is generally up to date and accurate, my endorsement doesn't mean I agree with everything that appears in these books or on these websites.

Alternative and Complementary Medicine
The National Center for Complementary and Integrative Medicine (www.nccih.nih.gov)
Accurate, up-to-date safety and efficacy information on specific herbs, supplements, and practices (such as acupuncture).

Domestic Violence and Sexual Abuse Support
Many people experience intimidation, threats, or even physical harm in their relationships or during contact with others, whether at home, outside, or at work. Here are some of the resources available to you regardless of your gender identity, race, age, citizenship status, or sexual orientation.
National Domestic Violence Hotline *1-800-799-SAFE*

National Human Trafficking Hotline *1-888-3737-888* or text *BEFREE to #233733*

Rape, Abuse, and Incest National Network (www.RAINN. org)

800-656-HOPE (800-656-4673)

The nation's largest anti-sexual-violence organization has thousands of trained volunteers available 24/7. Please note that if you call 1-800-656-HOPE, a computer will note your area code and the first three digits of your phone number.

Finding an Expert

The Northwestern Medicine Center for Sexual Medicine and Menopause (www.nm.org)

The Northwestern Medicine Center for Sexual Medicine and Menopause is the center I founded and oversee. Located in Chicago, it is part of Northwestern University and is staffed by experienced physicians, advanced practice nurses and physician assistants. All are certified menopause practitioners of the North American Menopause Society. We work collaboratively with other physicians, certified sex therapists, and pelvic floor physical therapists. We have programs for menopause, vulvar and vaginal health, bone health, and sexual function. It is worth the trip to Chicago.

The North American Menopause Society (NAMS) (www. menopause.org)

If you are not in Chicago, the North American Menopause Society's website is the place to go to find a certified menopause practitioner. On the homepage, click on the "For Women" tab at the top, then go to "Find a Menopause Practitioner." Once the list of providers in your ZIP code comes up, be aware that "NCMP" designates a NAMS certified menopause practitioner who has met specific criteria.

If someone is not certified, it means they have paid to be a member, and though they are interested enough in menopause to join NAMS, they have not passed the certification exam.

American Board of Medical Specialties (ABMS) (www. abms.org)

This organization oversees physician certification by developing standards for the evaluation and certification of physician specialists. Go to the ABMS website to find out whether a physician is board-certified.

Federation of State Medical Boards (FSMB) (www.fsmb. org)

Visit this website to verify that a physician is licensed.

General Medical Information

Check out chapter *Calling Dr. Google* for additional information about the following recommended websites.

Up To Date (www.uptodate.com)

General medical information for physicians and other health care professionals which requires a paid subscription, but there is also a free patient portal.

Mayo Clinic (www.mayoclinic.org)

This site is good for general medical information about specific symptoms, tests, and procedures.

PubMed (www.ncbi.nlm.nih.gov/pubmed)

This site is where medical journal articles are published. Sometimes the full article is available but sometimes it only gives a summary and redirects you to the journal website which requires a subscription for full access.

Pelvic Floor Physical Therapy

Pelvic Floor Physical therapists trained by Herman & Wallace Pelvic Rehabilitation Institute (www.pelvicrehab.com)

American Physical Therapy Association (APTA) Section on Women's Health (www.aptapelvichealth.org/ptlocator)

Relationship Books
Taking Sexy Back, by Alexandra Solomon, PhD

Loving Bravely, by Alexandra Solomon, PhD

Mating in Captivity: Reconciling the Erotic and the Domestic, by Ester Perel, PhD

Love Worth Making, by Stephen Snyder, MD

Come as You Are, by Emily Nagoski, PhD

Sex Therapists
American Association of Sex Educators, Counselors, and Therapists (AASECT) (www.aasect.org)

Sexual Pain and Sexual Health
Slip Sliding Away: Turning Back the Clock on Your Vagina-A gynecologist's guide to eliminating post-menopause dryness and pain by Lauren Streicher, MD

Sex Rx: Hormones, Health and Your Best Sex Ever, by Lauren Streicher, MD

When Sex Hurts: A Woman's Guide to Banishing Sexual Pain, by Andrew Goldstein, Caroline Pukall, and Irwin Goldstein

Pelvic Pain, Explained, by Stephanie A. Prendergast and Elizabeth H. Akincilar

International Pelvic Pain Society (www.pelvicpain.org)

Weight Control
Six Factors to Fit, by Robert Kushner, MD

Eat Like a Woman (and never diet again), by Staness Jonekos with Marjorie Jenkins, MD

Over-the-Counter Products
This section contains information on some of the over-the- counter products and devices mentioned in the Inside Information Series. No one paid to be mentioned in this book or included in this resources section. This is not meant to be a comprehensive list. Many products that are safe and effective are not included.

Hot Flash Relief
Relizen™ (www.hellobonafide.com/products/relizen)
Equelle™ (www.equelle.com)

Long-Acting Vaginal Moisturizers
Replens™ Long Lasting Vaginal Moisturizer polycarbophil-based moisturizer (www.replens.com)
Revaree™ hyaluronic acid-based moisturizer (www.hellobonafide.com/products/revaree)
Hyalo™ Gyn Gel hyaluronic acid-based moisturizer (www.hyalogyn.com)

Low Osmolality Water-Based Lubricants
World Health Organization:
Full list of osmolality of commercial vaginal lubricants: (apps.who.int/iris/bitstream/handle/10665/76580/WHO_RHR_12.33_eng.pdf;jsessionid=849958F8DB-CD902D1F23041BDE7C6776?sequence=1)
Good Clean Love™
System Jo™

Slippery Stuff ™
Pulse H2Oh! ™

Silicone Lubricants
Replens Silky Smooth
Pulse Aloe-ahh™
Wet Platinum™
JO™ Premium Personal Lubricant
PINK™ Silicone Lubricant
SLIQUID™ Organics silk

Vulvar Soothing Products
Aquaphor™ Healing Ointment (www.aquaphorus.com)
Replens ™Moisture Restore External Comfort Gel (www.replens.com)
Hyalo™ Gyn Gel (www.hyalogyn.com)

To Restore Normal Vaginal Ph
RePhresh™ (www.rephresh.com)
Replens Long Lasting Vaginal Moisturizer (www.replens.com)

Vaginal Dilators
Soul Source (www.soulsource.com)
Intimate Rose (www.IntimateRose.com)
Milli™, a single dilator that expands (www.milliforher.com)

Pelvic Floor-Strengthening Device
ATTAIN™ treats urinary and bowel incontinence (www.incontrolmedical.com).
GoodRx.com is a website that compares prices at neighborhood pharmacies and can send coupons to your phone **Full disclosure:** I have a financial relationship with this product, which has been clinically proven to reduce urinary urgency and stress incontinence and bowel incontinence.

19

TERMINOLOGY/GLOSSARY

THE FIRST SECTION of this glossary is a quick reference to basic definitions related to menopause. It is followed by terms used throughout my other books. Further information on each term can be found in the book listed next to it. If no book is listed, it means the book that digs deeper into that topic is not yet available.

Menopause Definitions

Early menopause. Although it is normal for a woman to go through menopause in her early 40s, it occurs spontaneously in only 3% to 5% of women and is considered to be an early menopause. Most early menopause is a consequence of surgery.

Induced menopause. This is menopause that occurs because of surgical removal of the ovaries or because of a cancer treatment, such as pelvic radiation or chemotherapy. Women who have an induced menopause do not go through perimenopause.

Menopause. Menopause is defined as the final menstrual period, which is confirmed once someone has not had a period for 12 months. Of course, for women who do not have periods (due to hysterectomy, uterine ablation, IUD), this is not a useful benchmark. Essentially, menopause is when the ovaries are no longer producing ovarian hormones, primarily estrogen. The average age of menopause in the United States is 52, but it is normal to enter menopause any time after age 40.

Perimenopause. This is the time leading up to menopause, when hormones start to fluctuate, and periods are unpredictably irregular. Any symptoms experienced during menopause can occur during perimenopause. Perimenopause can last weeks, months, or years, but it is officially over when a menstruating woman has been without a period for 12 months.

Post-menopause. This refers to life after you enter menopause. You are post-menopause until you die.

Premature menopause. This is menopause that occurs at or before the age of 40. In many cases, this is genetic, but it may also be the result of an autoimmune disease or have been induced by surgery or cancer treatments.

Premenopausal. Premenopause starts with puberty and continues until perimenopause. A 15-year-old is considered to be premenopause.

Primary ovarian insufficiency (POI). This is defined as when the ovaries wind down before the age of 40. It may be permanent, in which case it is premature menopause, or it may be temporary. POI is not the same as premature menopause. Premature menopause is permanent. In POI, ovarian activity kicks in again. This is common during cancer treatment.

Spontaneous (natural) menopause. This is menopause that is not caused by medical treatment, surgery, radiation, or chemotherapy.

Glossary of Terminology Used in the Inside Information Series

A

Anandamide (AEA). An endocannabinoid made in humans that, in addition to a number of other functions, *also helps regulate body temperature. Hot Flash Hell: A Gynecologist's Guide to Turning Down the Heat*

Androgens. Hormones, such as testosterone, androstenedione, and dehydroepiandrosterone (DHEA), that are associated with male sex characteristics and structures but are also produced in smaller quantities in women. Androgens play a role in sexual function, muscle mass, bone density, distribution of fat tissue, energy, and psychological well-being. In women, most androgen production is divided between the ovaries and adrenal glands. *Hot Flash Hell: A Gynecologist's Guide to Turning Down the Heat*

Androgenetic alopecia. Thinning of the hair on the scalp. Though common in peri- and post-menopausal women, the actual cause is unknown. Genetic predisposition, hormone levels, and stress all might be factors.

Anti-Mullerian Hormone (AMH). Blood levels of anti-Mullerian hormone have been used by fertility specialists for years to evaluate ovarian reserve—essentially, how good eggs are, and how long they will be functional. AMH declines with age as the "good" egg pool decreases and is completely gone after menopause. Sometimes AMH is used as a predictor for when someone is going to go into menopause because levels are known to drop roughly five years before menopause. But at this time, these measures are not reliable. *Hot Flash Hell: A Gynecologist's Guide to Turning Down the Heat*

Aromatase inhibitors. A class of prescription drugs used for the prevention and treatment of breast cancer. Aromatase inhibitors work by blocking the formation of estrogen in the body's tissues. *Hot Flash Hell: A Gynecologist's Guide to Turning Down the Heat*

B

Bazodoxifene (BZA). A selective estrogen receptor modulator (SERM) that helps protect the uterine lining from the thickening that may occur in women who take estrogen. *Hot Flash Hell: A Gynecologist's Guide to Turning Down the Heat*

Bilateral oophorectomy. Oophorectomy refers to the surgical removal of the ovaries. Bilateral specifies removal of both ovaries. T*he Essential Guide to Hysterectomy*

Bilateral salpingo-oophorectomy. The surgical removal of both the ovaries and fallopian tubes. *The Essential Guide to Hysterectomy*

C

Cannabidiol (CBD). CBD is extracted from hemp flowers. It does not have psychoactive properties, so it will not get you high. CBD contains trace amounts of THC. CBD may decrease pain and inflammation in addition to helping you get a good night's sleep. *Slip Sliding Away: Turning Back the Clock on Your Vagina; Hot Flash Hell: A Gynecologist's Guide to Turning Down the Heat*

Cholesterol. A fat-like substance used by the body to make hormones, vitamin D, and substances that help you digest foods. Cholesterol also is found in some foods.

Clonidine. A prescription drug that is FDA approved to lower high blood pressure but is sometimes prescribed off label to treat hot flashes. *Hot Flash Hell: A Gynecologist's Guide to Turning Down the Heat*

Commercially produced bioidentical estrogen. Plant-derived beta-estradiol, which is essentially identical to the estrogen produced by the ovaries. These products are FDA approved and are taken by mouth as a pill; transdermally as a patch, gel, or spray; or via a disposable vaginal ring. *Hot Flash Hell: A Gynecologist's Guide to Turning Down the Heat*

Congestive heart failure. A condition in which the heart is unable to maintain adequate circulation of blood in the body.

Conjugated estrogens (CE). A mixture of estrogen hormones used to treat symptoms of menopause, such as hot flashes, vaginal dryness, burning, and irritation. Other uses include the prevention of osteoporosis in post-menopausal women and the replacement of estrogen in women with ovarian failure or other conditions that cause a lack of natural estrogen in the body. *Slip Sliding Away: Turning Back the Clock on Your Vagina; Hot Flash Hell: A Gynecologist's Guide to Turning Down the Heat*

Coronary artery disease (CAD). Sometimes called coronary heart disease (CHD), this is the most common form of heart disease. CAD refers to damaged or diseased blood vessels that supply blood to the heart. See also cardiovascular disease (CVD).

Coronary heart disease (CHD). See coronary artery disease (CAD).

Compounded bioidentical estrogen. Plant-derived beta-estradiol, which is essentially identical to the estrogen produced by the ovaries and identical to the estradiol in commercial products. Compounded products are not FDA approved and are distributed by independent compounding pharmacies. Compounded estrogen is administered through the skin as a lotion or gel, or via a pellet placed under the skin. *Hot Flash Hell: A Gynecologist's Guide to Turning Down the Heat*

Commercially produced conjugated or synthetic estrogen. Conjugated estrogens are mixtures of manmade or natural estrogens. *Synthetic estrogen or conjugated estrogens* are derived from a plant source. *Conjugated equine estrogen* is composed of multiple estrogens derived from the urine of pregnant horses. Most of these products are now off the market due to the emergence of bioidentical products. *Hot Flash Hell: A Gynecologist's Guide to Turning Down the Heat*

Cystitis. Inflammation of the urinary bladder. See also urinary tract infection.

Cystocele. Protrusion of the urinary bladder. *The Essential Guide to Hysterectomy*

D

Dehydroepiandrosterone (DHEA). An androgen produced mainly in the adrenal glands. It is a precursor of androstenedione, testosterone, and estrogen. DHEA decreases with age, not menopause. *Slip Sliding Away: Turning Back the Clock on Your Vagina*

Dyspareunia. Pain during intercourse. *Slip Sliding Away: Turning Back the Clock on Your Vagina; Sex Rx: Hormones, Health and Your Best Sex Ever*

E

Endocannabinoid receptors. Required for endocannabinoids to become active. **CB1 receptors** are mostly found in the central nervous system (brain and spinal cord) but are also in the reproductive system, heart, lungs, skin, and adrenal glands. **CB2 receptors** are found in the liver, bones, spleen, digestive tract, peripheral nervous system, and immune system. *Hot Flash Hell: A Gynecologist's Guide to Turning Down the Heat*

Endocannabinoid system. A complex nerve-signaling system composed of neurotransmitters that bind to cannabinoid receptors. It is responsible for regulating multiple body functions, including appetite, metabolism, pain, mood, learning, memory, sleep, bone health, cardiovascular health, and stress. *Hot Flash Hell: A Gynecologist's Guide to Turning Down the Heat*

Endometrial ablation. A surgical procedure in which heat energy is used to destroy the lining (endometrium) of the uterus to treat heavy bleeding. *The Essential Guide to Hysterectomy*

Endometrial biopsy. A sample of endometrial (uterine lining) tissue is removed through the opening of the cervix and examined microscopically for abnormal cells. *The Essential Guide to Hysterectomy*

Endometrial cancer. Cancer of the inner lining (endometrium) of the uterus. *The Essential Guide to Hysterectomy*

Endometrial hyperplasia. An overgrowth of tissue or a thickening of the uterine lining often caused by excess estrogen. It is a risk factor for cancer of the uterus. *Hot Flash Hell: A Gynecologist's Guide to Turning Down the Heat; The Essential Guide to Hysterectomy*

Endometrium. The tissue that lines the cavity of the uterus.

Estradiol. Also called 17β-estradiol. It is the most potent of the naturally occurring estrogens and the primary estrogen produced by the ovaries during the reproductive years. *Hot Flash Hell: A Gynecologist's Guide to Turning Down the Heat*

Estriol. The least potent of the estrogens produced in the body.

Estrogen. Hormone compounds produced by the ovaries. The three main naturally occurring estrogens in women are estradiol, estrone, and estriol.

Estrone. A weak form of estrone is produced in the ovaries and fat.

Estrogen therapy (ET). A general term describing systemic and local formulations in oral, skin patch, and vaginal prescriptions. ET specifically refers to hormone therapy that does not include a progestogen. See also systemic estrogen therapy, local estrogen therapy. *Slip Sliding Away: Turning Back the Clock on Your Vagina; Hot Flash Hell: A Gynecologist's Guide to Turning Down the Heat*

F

Fibrinogen. A protein in the blood that helps it clot.

Follicle-stimulating hormone (FSH). A hormone produced by the pituitary gland, which is located at the base of the brain. FSH stimulates production of estrogen by the ovaries and, during the reproductive years, stimulates the growth of ovarian follicles (the small cysts that hold the eggs). During perimenopause, FSH levels fluctuate. Once a woman has entered menopause and estrogen production has ceased, FSH levels remain high. *Hot Flash Hell: A Gynecologist's Guide to Turning Down the Heat*

Formication. Many perimenopausal women experience skin sensations such as itching or the feeling that there are "ants crawling" on their skin. This phenomenon is known as formication.

G

Gabapentin. A nonhormonal prescription drug usually prescribed for the treatment of seizures but sometimes prescribed off label for treating hot flashes. *Hot Flash Hell: A Gynecologist's Guide to Turning Down the Heat*

Genitourinary syndrome of menopause (GSM). A group of symptoms and signs associated with menopause that can involve changes to the labia, clitoris, vagina, urethra, and bladder. *Slip Sliding Away: Turning Back the Clock on Your Vagina*

Gonadotropin-releasing hormone (GnRH). A hormone released by the hypothalamus (a region in the brain) that inhibits ovarian production of estrogen.

H

High-density lipoprotein cholesterol (HDL-C). Referred to as the "good" cholesterol. High HDL-C helps to lower the risk of heart disease.

Hormone therapy (HT). Prescription drugs to treat menopause symptoms. HT may include estrogen, progestogen, and sometimes testosterone. *Slip Sliding Away: Turning Back the Clock on Your Vagina; Hot Flash Hell: A Gynecologist's Guide to Turning Down the Heat*

Husband replacement therapy (HRT). In addition to HT, often necessary for sexual satisfaction and quality of life. *Slip Sliding Away: Turning Back the Clock on Your Vagina; Hot Flash Hell: A Gynecologist's Guide to Turning Down the Heat*

Hybrid cannabis. A hybrid cannabis plant has aspects of indica and sativa. The interbreeding of these hybrid strains has become so common that some say the unique distinctions between indica and sativa no longer exist. *Hot Flash Hell: A Gynecologist's Guide to Turning Down the Heat*

Hypertension. Abnormally high blood pressure.

Hypoactive sexual desire disorder (HSDD). Problems with sexual desire, arousal, orgasmic response, and sexual pain. Between one-third and one-half of perimenopausal and post-menopausal women experience these problems. *Sex Rx: Hormones, Health and Your Best Sex Ever*

Hysterectomy. Surgical removal of the uterus. Does not result in menopause but ends menstrual periods and fertility. The term is often mistakenly used to describe the removal of the uterus and both ovaries, which results in surgical menopause. *The Essential Guide to Hysterectomy*

Hysteroscopy. A surgical procedure to examine the inside of the uterus by inserting a thin, lighted tube into the vagina and through the cervix (the lower, narrow end of the uterus). *The Essential Guide to Hysterectomy*

I

Incontinence. Involuntary loss of urine or stool. The Essential Guide to Hysterectomy; *Sex Rx: Hormones, Health and Your Best Sex Ever; Slip Sliding Away: Turning Back the Clock on Your Vagina*

Indica. This species of cannabis comes from a short, bushy plant and is anecdotally known for its calming attributes. Indica is used for pain relief, sleep, and relaxation and is best taken at night. *Hot Flash Hell: A Gynecologist's Guide to Turning Down the Heat*

Intrauterine device (IUD). Also called an intrauterine system (IUS). A small device with either progestin or copper that is placed in the uterus by a healthcare provider. Though primarily used for contraception, the levonorgestrol IUD is also used to control perimenopausal heavy bleeding and, off label, to protect the uterine lining in a woman taking post-menopause estrogen therapy. *Hot Flash Hell: A Gynecologist's Guide to Turning Down the Heat*

Isoflavones. Naturally occurring, estrogen-like compounds found in soybeans, soy products, and red clover.

Hot Flash Hell: A Gynecologist's Guide to Turning Down the Heat

L

Lichen sclerosus. A condition that causes thinning of the vulvar skin along with symptoms such as itching, burning, and painful sexual activity. Treatment is regular surveillance and topical corticosteroids. There is an association of lichen sclerosus with vulvar cancer. *Sex Rx: Hormones, Health and Your Best Sex Ever*

Local vaginal estrogens. Creams, tablets, vaginal rings, inserts, or suppositories placed in the vagina to specifically alleviate the symptoms of vaginal atrophy and genitourinary syndrome of menopause. Although some vaginal estrogen is absorbed into the bloodstream, the amount is minimal, and its effects are local rather than systemic. For that reason, vaginal estrogen has no impact on your hot flashes, bones, or brain. *Slip Sliding Away: Turning Back the Clock on Your Vagina*

Low-density lipoprotein cholesterol (LDL-C). The "bad" cholesterol. Elevated LDL-C increases the risk of heart disease. *Hot Flash Hell: A Gynecologist's Guide to Turning Down the Heat*

Luteinizing hormone (LH). A hormone produced by the pituitary gland (located at the base of the brain) that triggers the release of an egg from the ovary (ovulation). LH levels rise during menopause. *Hot Flash Hell: A Gynecologist's Guide to Turning Down the Heat*

M

Metabolic syndrome. A condition characterized by the presence of three or more of the following factors: central obesity (increased waist circumference), elevated triglyceride levels, low HDL-C, elevated blood pressure, and/or an elevated fasting glucose level. Women with metabolic syndrome are at increased risk for heart disease, stroke, and type 2 diabetes (adult-onset diabetes).

N

NAMS menopause practitioner. A licensed healthcare clinician who has achieved a certification in the field of menopause from the North American Menopause Society by passing a competency examination. *Slip Sliding Away: Turning Back the Clock on Your Vagina; Hot Flash Hell: A Gynecologist's Guide to Turning Down the Heat*

Nonsteroidal anti-inflammatory drugs (NSAIDs). A class of non-narcotic, over-the-counter drugs that provides painkilling, fever-reducing, and, in higher doses, anti-inflammatory effects. Examples of commonly used NSAIDS are aspirin, ibuprofen, and naproxen.

O

Off label. Refers to the use of a drug to treat a condition for which it has not been FDA approved. *Slip Sliding Away: Turning Back the Clock on Your Vagina; Hot Flash Hell: A Gynecologist's Guide to Turning Down the Heat*

Ospemifene. An oral medication used to treat vaginal dryness and painful intercourse. It is a selective estrogen receptor modulator (SERM). *Slip Sliding Away: Turning Back the Clock on Your Vagina*

P

Paroxetine. A selective serotonin reuptake inhibitor (SSRI) used to treat depressive and general anxiety disorders. Low-dose paroxetine is FDA approved for the treatment of hot flashes. Higher doses are sometimes used off label to treat flashes. *Slip Sliding Away: Turning Back the Clock on Your Vagina; Hot Flash Hell: A Gynecologist's Guide to Turning Down the Heat*

Phytocannabinoids. A cannabinoid extracted from the marijuana plant, aka cannabis. *Hot Flash Hell: A Gynecologist's Guide to Turning Down the Heat*

Phytoestrogens. Plant compounds (such as isoflavones) that have a chemical structure similar to that of estrogen and have weak, estrogen-like biologic activity. Available in foods (such as soy) and as nonprescription supplements. See also isoflavones. *Hot Flash Hell: A Gynecologist's Guide to Turning Down the Heat*

Placebo. An inactive substance used in controlled experiments to determine the effectiveness of a drug or other substance in comparison. *Slip Sliding Away: Turning Back the Clock on Your Vagina; Hot Flash Hell: A Gynecologist's Guide to Turning Down the Heat*

Progesterone. The naturally occurring hormone normally produced by the ovaries after a woman ovulates. *Hot Flash Hell: A Gynecologist's Guide to Turning Down the Heat*

Progestin. Any *synthetic* form of progesterone. Progestins are commonly used in hormonal forms of contraception, such as birth control pills, implants, and IUDs, but they are also used in lower doses for menopause hormone therapy. Progestins used in FDA-approved products include *drospirenone, levonorgestrel,* medroxyprogesterone acetate (MPA), *norethindrone* acetate, and *norgestinate. Hot Flash Hell: A Gynecologist's Guide to Turning Down the Heat*

Progestogen. A general term that includes all compounds that bind to progesterone receptors. Progestogens include *both* naturally occurring progesterone and synthetic progestins. *Hot Flash Hell: A Gynecologist's Guide to Turning Down the Heat*

S

Sativa. The sativa species of cannabis is a tall, slim plant. It is often used during the day because it is purported to boost energy, increase focus, and be overall stimulating instead of sedating. *Hot Flash Hell: A Gynecologist's Guide to Turning Down the Heat*

Selective estrogen-receptor modulator (SERM). A compound that has a similar chemical structure to estrogen and either blocks estrogen receptors or stimulates them. SERMs can have an estrogen-like effect on some tissues and an antiestrogen effect on others. *Slip Sliding Away: Turning Back the Clock on Your Vagina; Hot Flash Hell: A Gynecologist's Guide to Turning Down the Heat*

Selective serotonin-reuptake inhibitor (SSRI). A commonly prescribed class of antidepressants that blocks the reabsorption (reuptake) of the neurotransmitter serotonin in the brain. SSRIs are often used off label to treat hot flashes. *Hot Flash Hell: A Gynecologist's Guide to Turning Down the Heat*

Selective norepinephrine-reuptake inhibitor (SNRI). A commonly prescribed class of antidepressants that blocks the reabsorption (reuptake) of the neurotransmitter norepinephrine in the brain. SNRIs are often used off label to treat hot flashes. *Hot Flash Hell: A Gynecologist's Guide to Turning Down the Heat*

Stress incontinence. Involuntary loss of urine that occurs when someone coughs, sneezes, laughs, or exercises. *Slip Sliding Away: Turning Back the Clock on Your Vagina; The*

Essential Guide to Hysterectomy; Sex Rx: Hormones, Health and Your Best Sex Ever

Study of Women's Health Across the Nation (SWAN). A study of over 3,000 midlife women that started in 1994 and is ongoing. Caucasian (46%), Black (28%), Hispanic (9%), and Asian (17%) American women between the ages of 40 and 55 from all over the country were enrolled in order to study midlife health, the impact of menopause, and hormone therapy. The data continues to roll in, and more than any other study, it has informed us about the impact of menopause and hormones on health. SWAN data also includes the effects of smoking, diet, medications, hormone therapy, and multiple psychosocial variables. Much of the information in the Inside Information Series is derived from SWAN. If you would like to take a look at this information yourself, all of the data is published on the SWAN website (www.swanstudy.org). *Hot Flash Hell: A Gynecologist's Guide to Turning Down the Heat*

Systemic estrogen therapy. Estrogen therapy that works throughout the body to alleviate symptoms such as hot flashes. The blood level you achieve with estrogen therapy is not intended to be as high as when you were 20 (which is why it is called estrogen therapy or hormone therapy, as opposed to estrogen replacement therapy or hormone replacement therapy) but high enough to alleviate symptoms. A systemic estrogen may be oral (a pill), or it may be transmitted through the skin (transdermal) in the form of a spray, patch, gel, or cream. One vaginal product, Femring™, delivers systemic-level doses in the same range as transdermal and oral products. *Hot Flash Hell: A Gynecologist's Guide to Turning Down the Heat*

T

Tamoxifen. A prescription selective estrogen-receptor modulator (SERM) that is prescribed for the prevention and treatment of breast cancer in high-risk women. *Slip Sliding Away: Turning Back the Clock on Your Vagina; Hot Flash Hell: A Gynecologist's Guide to Turning Down the Heat*

Testosterone. A hormone essential for sperm production, secondary sex characteristics, and other functions in men. In women, testosterone contributes to lubrication and libido, and it may also help maintain bone and muscle health. *Slip Sliding Away: Turning Back the Clock on Your Vagina; Hot Flash Hell: A Gynecologist's Guide to Turning Down the Heat; Sex Rx: Hormones, Health and Your Best Sex Ever*

Tetrahydrocannabinol (THC). The psychoactive component of cannabis. It activates CB1 receptors and can create a euphoric feeling. THC mimics some aspects of anandamide, the endocannabinoid that helps regulate body temperature, which is theoretically why THC may be the key to reducing hot flashes. *Hot Flash Hell: A Gynecologist's Guide to Turning Down the Heat*

Transdermal estrogen. Estrogen therapy delivered through the skin into the bloodstream via a skin patch or topical lotion, spray, cream, or gel. *Hot Flash Hell: A Gynecologist's Guide to Turning Down the Heat*

U

Urge incontinence. Involuntary leakage of urine accompanied by a sense of urgency. *Slip Sliding Away: Turning Back the Clock on Your Vagina*

Urinary incontinence. Involuntary loss of urine. See also incontinence, stress incontinence, urge incontinence. *Slip*

Sliding Away: Turning Back the Clock on Your Vagina; The Essential Guide to Hysterectomy; Sex Rx: Hormones, Health and Your Best Sex Ever

Urinary tract infection (UTI). Sometimes called cystitis, a UTI is when bacteria in the urinary tract cause infection and inflammation. Typical symptoms are urgency and pain with urination. *Slip Sliding Away: Turning Back the Clock on Your Vagina*

Urogynecologist. A gynecologist with additional training in incontinence and pelvic relaxation problems, such as prolapse. *Slip Sliding Away: Turning Back the Clock on Your Vagina*

V

Vaginal estrogen therapy. See local estrogen therapy

Vaginal atrophy. A condition in which estrogen loss causes the tissues of the vulva (the external parts of the female genital organs) and the lining of the vagina to become thin, dry, and less elastic. See also genitourinary syndrome of menopause. *Slip Sliding Away: Turning Back the Clock on Your Vagina*

Vaginal estrogen. Prescription estrogen therapy that is applied vaginally (as a cream, ring, suppository, or tablet) to treat vaginal dryness and atrophy. Most vaginal estrogen therapies provide local, not systemic, treatment. See also local therapy. *Slip Sliding Away: Turning Back the Clock on Your Vagina*

Vaginal lubricant. Over-the-counter products applied to the opening of the vagina to decrease friction and reduce pain during intercourse. *Slip Sliding Away: Turning Back the Clock on Your Vagina*

Vaginal moisturizer. Over-the-counter products that increase the water content of vaginal cells to increase lubrication and elasticity. Moisturizers are intended to be used on a regular basis in anticipation of sexual activity. *Slip Sliding Away: Turning Back the Clock on Your Vagina*

Vasomotor symptoms. Commonly known as hot flashes, vasomotor symptoms specifically refer to changes in the diameter of blood vessels that cause a change in body temperature and speed up your heart rate. *Hot Flash Hell: A Gynecologist's Guide to Turning Down the Heat*

Vulva. The external parts of the female genitalia, including the tissue around the opening of the vagina. *Slip Sliding Away: Turning Back the Clock on Your Vagina*

W

Women's Health Initiative (WHI). A large study that looked at the impact of oral estrogen on cardiovascular disease, stroke, breast cancer, osteoporosis, colon cancer, and other conditions. *Hot Flash Hell: A Gynecologist's Guide to Turning Down the Heat*

ACKNOWLEDGMENTS

I DECIDED NOT to go the traditional route when publishing the *Dr. Streicher's Inside Information* series. I have been very lucky as an author and have always had a literary agent and a publisher willing to pay me an advance, edit, format, and market my books. But in exchange for those advantages, there is something every author gives up when working with a traditional publishing house: control. Once the book is sold, it is the publisher's call what the author can, should, and must include.

I admit I am a little bit of a control freak, whether it is in the operating room or in the kitchen. With *Dr. Streicher's Inside Information* series, I decided I wanted to do it my way. Even the most talented editor or publisher does not have what I have—30 years of experience running a menopause clinic and listening to the concerns of thousands of women from all over the country as I take care of them.

I also would like to emphasize that although many products are recommended, no one paid to be mentioned in this book. When it comes to prescription products, I included every FDA-approved option available at the time of publication.

There are a number of other people who made this series possible.

Thank you to my dear friend **Rick Kogan** for introducing me to **Joe Darrow**, who is responsible for the fabulous cover designs and all of the Francey images. Check out his website, joedarrow.com, to see his iconic magazine covers.

The talented **Telisha Bryan**, copy editor extraordinaire, who fixed too many typos and errors to count after I gave her what I considered to be "a ready-to-go, perfect manuscript." For any writer who doesn't think you need a copy editor, you are wrong.

Rachel Zar, my brilliant daughter, is a much better writer than I will ever be. She is also a talented marital and family therapist, and an ASSECT-certified sex therapist. I have the pleasure of working with her in the Northwestern Medicine Center for Sexual Medicine and Menopause. Rachel reviewed the copy, edited out the bad stuff, and gave me the kind of advice most daughters never have to give their mothers.

The world of cannabis was completely new to me, and I am grateful to my friend **Jim Belushi** for introducing me to the nuances of cannabis as medicine. He let me hang out on Belushi's Farm and eat cannabis-infused chocolate. Check out the Discovery Channel series *Growing Belushi* and see if you can spot my cameo appearance!

Luba Andrus, RPh, MJ, is a cannabis expert, clinical educational coordinator, and pharmacist in the state of Illinois who provided information on the specifics of alleviating menopause symptoms. She continues to be a great source of information about the nuances of using cannabis for relief.

I met **Suzy Ginsberg** years ago, when I did a commercial for a tampon that eliminated vaginal odor. The vagina talk and laughter have never stopped. Not only has she become my one-woman support group, but I also count her among my dearest friends.

Lorraine Devon Wilke, a friend and talented author (check out her books on Amazon!), was a wealth of information regarding the intricacies of publishing.

Francey O., my childhood friend, whom my character is not based on (other than the smart and witty part) for letting me borrow her name.

I am terrible at social media. I forget to post, I forget to tag, I forget to link. I still can't figure out Instagram—forget TikTok. It took me awhile to admit it (I am one of those people who have a hard time admitting they are bad at anything) and agree to hire someone who could do it right. So far, I have hired three social media people, and each one disappeared after a few months. I am optimistic that I will find someone who can help me get out there on Facebook, Twitter, Instagram, YouTube, and LinkedIn. So thank you to every single person who follows me on social media despite my posting problems and keeps the conversation about menopause alive and relevant.

To **Brad Ginsberg** and all the folks at Global Communications Works. There are a lot of PR companies. This is a company that not only understands the world of vaginal health but is also better than anyone else at getting out the word. Thank you!

My patients continue to inform me. It's one thing to make recommendations based on the scientific literature, but it is the real-life experiences of the women who use these products that give me the real education.

A special shout out to my colleagues at the Northwestern Medicine Center for Sexual Medicine and Menopause: **Traci Kurtzer, MD; Kristi Tough DeSapri, MD; Rajal Patel, MD; Pat Handler, MSN FPN-C; Sarah Hwang, MD; Audrey Fenwick, MS, PA-C; Rachel Zar, MS, LFMT, CST; Jennifer Levy, MA, LCPC; Toshiko Odaira, PT, DPT; and Helene Strange, PT, DPT, OCS.** They are all extraordinary clinicians who are responsible for the success of our programs.

I am lucky to be part of an amazing group of academic menopause experts. Every non-pandemic year, we gather at the North American Menopause Society conference and drink, eat, drink, laugh, drink, and, yes, share information about updates in research and clinical practice. All of these folks are my go-to sources and collectively know so much more than I will ever know: **Risa Kagan, MD; Pauline Maki, PhD; Lisa Larkin, MD; Stephanie Faubian, MD; James Simon, MD; Marla Shapiro, MD; Jan Shifren, MD; Andrew Goldstein, MD; David Portman, MD; Leah Milheiser, MD; Sharon Parrish, MD; Sheryl Kingsberg, PhD; Rebecca Thurston, PhD; Mary Jane Minken, MD; Tara Allman, MD; Diana Bitner, MD; Brian Bernick, MD; Miriam Greene, MD; and Nicole Jaff, PhD.** (Sorry if I forgot anyone!)

A special thank you to **Pauline Maki, PhD,** renowned for her groundbreaking work on menopause and cognitive function, for reviewing the section on hot flashes and the brain.

To our daughters **Rachel, Danielle, Jessie,** and **Julian,** my brothers, **Paul, Michael,** and **Ian,** and my sisters-in-law, **Liz, and Kim,** who proudly display my vagina books in their homes. I am so lucky to have family whom I not only love but truly like.

And, finally, to **Jason,** whom I adore more every day. In addition to being the best husband ever, Jason is a talented writer, musician, and composer. He wrote the music and lyrics for Francey's theme song. You can hear it on Youtube.com/DrStreicherTV. And while you are there, check out our new YouTube series, *Men-On-Pause*.

INDEX

THE SAGA OF FRANCEY'S JOURNEY through menopause continues!

Made in the USA
Las Vegas, NV
25 September 2021

31129117R00154